This is one of the
most inspirational book
I've eever read
Hope you enjoy it!

Glenn Gary
The Psychology of Higher Living
The Five Keys to Unlocking Your Greatest Life

BY GLENN GARY

OakStreet Press ISBN: 0-9774893-0-2

Glenn Gary

The Psychology of Higher Living

The Five Keys to Unlocking Your Greatest Life

Published By

www.oakstreetpress.com

Los Angeles   New York   London

As we walk through the valley of ordinary existence, who among us will strive to reach the mountaintop of higher living? In so striving, we transcend, overcome our adversity, seek a greater meaning to our lives, and unlock our greatest potential in the process. This should be our primary mission.

Regardless of whether you are sitting in the comforts of a mansion or reading this from the dark solitude of your car as you stare down homelessness, you are on a journey of a thousand miles. You have taken the first steps; acceptance of who you are and what has happened to you along the way is the evolution of your state of higher living.

Glenn Gary

Our lives represent the greatest dream and greatest hope that a man or woman has for our ability to be and our ability to accomplish; it is in this spirit that I present this book to you.

CONTENTS:

The Psychology of Higher Living
The Five Keys to Unlocking Your Greatest Life

Part 1:

Basic Human Development & Needs...35

Part 2:

Unconscious Living...79

PART 3:

Developing a Prosperity Consciousness...165

PART 4:

Developing a Greater Health Consciousness...205

Contents

PART 5:

The Path to Enlightenment...233

A FOUNDATION FOR HIGHER LIVING

The signpost up ahead tells you that life can be what-ever you decide to make it. The question then becomes, are you aware enough in your walk through life to even notice this truth? Life is full of choice points. Many choose to live in a determined state of igno-rance, unwilling to explore themselves more fully and risk the possibility of higher living. So who said igno-rance is bliss? I would suggest that ignorance just prevents people from enjoying their true potential.

Glenn Gary

One of my favorite quotes about the struggle of life is by Dr. Martin Luther King. He stated: *"I must confess that I have enjoyed being on this mountaintop and I am tempted to want to stay here and retreat to a more quiet and serene life. But something within reminds me that the valley calls me in spite of all its agonies, dangers and frustrating moments. I must return to the valley. Something tells me that the ultimate test of a man is not where he stands in moments of comfort and moments of convenience, but where he stands in moments of challenge and moments of contro-versy."*

Looking back over the landscape of my life, much like Dr. King, I too have been in many deep valleys. One cannot advise others until he himself has struggled, failed, overcome great obstacles, and risen again as a success. It is that struggle that has inspired me to question everything about life and reality as we know it. In this process, higher living mandates that we seek a greater enlightenment for our walk in life.

Why do some of us get stuck chasing after the satisfaction of our basic needs, spending all of our time on basic survival, food, money, sex, shelter, and water, while others seem to be at a much higher level of consciousness? They no longer spend their time tending the garden of basic needs and have moved on to a higher sense of living, of awareness, of purpose.

I believe that this life of higher awareness, if we choose to pursue it, will bring us the desired results of greater personal development and yet, sadly, many choose – key word *choose* – to operate at a lower level of consciousness, which is why we have millions of adults who are obese and millions of Americans addicted to drugs and alcohol.

My own adult life has been spent on my own journey of higher living, personal discovery, and greater awareness of what makes some people adopt better choices while others choose to self-sabotage and ultimately self destruct. I was forced to undertake this journey just to survive, to deal with the overwhelming grief that visited me during the summer of 1987. On a warm June evening, as I drove the vehicle that would ultimately kill my best childhood friend, my journey was about to begin. But like many of you, I was not defined by one incident in life, by one tragedy. We are a collective result of all experiences.

Walt Disney once wrote that there are three kinds of people in life, "well-poisoners," "lawnmowers," and "life-enrichers." He went on to say "well-poisoners" are the negative types who put other people down and try to discourage them from achieving their dreams. These are people who should be avoided and whose advice should be ignored. "Lawnmowers" are good citizens who keep up their own yards but seldom venture beyond their back fence. They go to work each day, pay their bills and taxes, obey the laws, and maintain their property but seldom volunteer or get involved in their community.

Then there are "life-enrichers." These are the people who really make life worth living. They go out of their way to enhance and enrich the lives of others with encouraging words and deeds. I knew as time went by and I overcame greater adversity that I wanted to be a life enricher, but little did I know how much the world would resist that desire. I realize that all of us, to fully unlock our greatest potential, to unleash our brilliance on the world, will need to thrive in spite of the many well-poisoners along the path.

Adversity is one of life's greatest teachers, and yet many people choose to deal with great adversity in one of two ways. Some people continue down the path of unconscious living, engaging in denial and self-sabotaging behavior and developing needless addictions to numb the pain of life's events. Others simply absorb the pain, allowing great loss or tragedy to be their guide, one that fills them with wisdom and strength.

This is not an easy road, to be sure, but as we will explore further, it's one that I believe will enable us to fully achieve a state of self-actualization and enlightenment. It will provide us with the knowledge to move past the desire to satiate our basic needs so that we can attain a higher level of living.

In the study of the human condition, modern psychology has given us a framework, an operating system if you will. At the beginning of this book we will explore this framework further. In addition, modern man must look to the past. In doing so, we could not acknowledge the totality of man's being if we did not recognize what is in my view our ability for achieving a state of what I call existential enlightenment. As I propagate to you my theory of the six stages of human development, I will expand on the tenets of existentialism further. As man searches for a greater meaning to his life, one must ask the following set of questions:

What operating system controls the basic criminal, as opposed to the wealthy business person? Why do some of us commit suicide when life throws us a curve ball, while others soak up these bad events and seem to grow stronger from them?

At the age of 13, while my parents were in the midst of divorcing after 17 years of what could be described as a miserable union at best, I was relocated to a facility for troubled teens. As my mother pulled up to the building, I was surrounded by four men. Not having any idea what was happening, I made a short run for it, but was quickly slammed to the ground, picked up, and hauled into the facility.

It would be almost one year before I was released. Needless to say that year was full of plenty of drama. In looking back on that forced incarceration, I remember how imperative it was to move up the levels that the facility had designated in order to "win" my release. New arrivals were placed on level R, which was lockdown, and there was no way to leave the place. This was not your kid's summer camp. Over a period of months, inmates could graduate to level 5 and be released to the reality of what they had left, assuming they were not suicidal or psychotic. Fortunately, I was neither one of those.

Some 25 years later, I have come to understand that there are six stages of human development. The more I lived through each one of these stages and struggled to push through and reach the next one, the more I was able to transcend my old reality and replace it with a new one—not that I forgot the past, but rather that my past, once fully accepted, would be my bridge to the future. Acceptance is the very biggest, and for many, the most difficult of life's hurdles.

Perhaps like many people, my past has been filled with tremendous sadness, and yet the world of today and indeed the future is so bright, illuminated with whatever possibilities my own mind can conceive. But this bright future can be for all of us; it's one that we can choose. It is this study of the human condition, my own and yours alike, that has brought me down this road to shine a light on why some of us fail so miserably in our marriages, our careers and our health, and how we can turn the ship around, change our life's course and sail to a better place.

I believe that each generation has thousands of people who achieve this greater sense of purpose and identity. Each generation has a small percentage of people that move through stages of lower living and reach a higher level of awareness, existential enlightenment and self-actualization. In essence, they are operating with better health, improved relationships, and more rewarding careers, and they have risen above the basic need for survival. I have often thought that life can be a waste if we are burdened with the constant thoughts of how we are going to make money to pay the bills.

This constant preoccupation with our own basic survival robs us of the ability to unlock our true potential. We cannot even begin to unlock the creative juices that enable us to move past adversity and create new careers, develop new skill sets, and move away from dysfunctional relationships—marriages where one person seems to have control of the "purse strings" and the other subordinates his or her own development, for example. If we do not have an abundance of meaningful love in our lives, then we tend to spend large amounts of our time trying to fill this need. If we are constantly struggling for money, most of our waking hours will be spent trying to find a way to earn more of it. When one of our basic needs has not been satisfied, it now becomes our innermost dominant need.

My philosophy of living started to take shape for me

in my early twenties, where I was constantly preoccupied with survival. I moved from job to job, from one apartment to the next in a very nomadic type of existence. The old saying, "that which does not kill us makes us stronger," applied to me perfectly. I did not allow myself to dwell on the significant tragedies of my youth; I often wondered why that was. As the years have gone by I realized that my ability to self-actualize gave me the ability to transcend the nightmare that was my past.

I submit to you that as we explore the six levels of human development and what it really means to become fully functional adults, you will begin to gain the clarity that will allow you to experience a reality that is magnificent and full of the endless possibilities, and in the process you will begin to raise your consciousness. I will attempt to guide you through this very large task by sharing with you some of the many experiences of unconscious living that I have been fortunate enough to survive along the way. As many of us realize, some of life's greatest lessons cost us dearly; we pay for them with blood, with the loss of a loved one, with money, or with our future.

Moreover, I am excited by the fact that there is a mentally stable stratum of our population that seeks greater enlightenment. I can only hope that we seek a sustained enlightenment if we are to fully absorb lasting change in our lives. I also recognize that a large percentage of our modern society chooses to dwell in a bewildering state of self-induced ignorance. What remains is the ashes of a life that is lived by accident in a reality not of our liking, but certainly of our choosing. Many people seem to cavil at the thought of discovering themselves further. This becomes an alarming state of consciousness that we must seek to eradicate if we are going to live a life of deep and lasting satisfaction.

Through this process of self-actualized existential enlightenment I have come to realize that all of us have something in common. Regardless of how wealthy we may be, or how broke we are, whether we're enjoying great health or are severely and dangerously overweight, whether we enjoy wonderful, healthy relationships or seem to be "trapped" in the most dysfunctional nightmares masquerading as a relationship, one thing that binds all of us is that we all feel good or even excited about some parts of our lives, and yet we all have parts of our lives that we want to improve, that we wish could be more fulfilling.

Recently I had a chance to talk with a 23-year-old woman who made a comment about the wonderful book that she was reading. I asked her, "So you like to read?" She replied emphatically, "I love to read." As I enquired further, I learned that it was a mystery suspense novel. I asked if she would be interested in reading my book when it was complete. She replied, "I hate self help books." I asked her why she enjoyed reading a book that was pure fiction; what could be learned from such a book? She simply stated, "Nothing. It just helps me take my mind off of my reality." She added, "I don't need to read a self help book because I am okay and not messed up, and besides, none of them are any good, anyway." I asked the young woman what part of her life she was most dissatisfied with. She replied, "I really hate my finances; I hate the career position that I am in." The issues behind her contradictory statements are part of the purpose of my book and why I have identified five basic areas of life that we must take hold of and learn more about, finances being one of the big areas. This is more than just another "self help" book. I will attempt to dissect and illuminate several key areas that we all inhabit. If one of them is clearly not working for us, it tends to dominate our thoughts and our time.

Without understanding the hierarchy of needs and the six stages of human development, you are living a life by accident, existing one day to the next. While many people spend hundreds of hours planning weddings or writing business plans to start a new company, I also have found that many of us put little time into understanding the reasons behind the choices we make every day and the fact that our reality as we know it is really the sum total of these choices. What we have chosen to focus on last week and last month dictates the reality of today.

Man's proclivity towards existential despair leads him to a sustained level of anxiety. This much we know, but our walk through life is one of great freedom and choice. Our ability to freely choose what levels of consciousness we inhabit is there for the taking. In the words of 19th century philosopher, Soren Kierkegaard, "Anxiety is the dizziness of freedom." The existential viewpoint of modern man's existence has seemed to largely fade from view over the past fifty years, although many of these existential themes are still prevalent in movies and books today. I am suggesting however that we revisit and possibly upgrade our understanding of the existential view and what it means to live in a post 9-11 twenty-first century world. A cultural epoch exists in our modern world that in part seems preoccupied with the potential nuclear threats from Iran and North Korea. Included in this equation is whether we will ever catch Bin Laden; it also includes an energy crises that not only chokes our environment, but also our wallets. In so doing, we will illuminate a greater awareness for our walk through life and the changes that we desire. Under the cloak of this new found insight, compassion and reason, we will shed new light on our most sacred dogmas. In the process we will understand more fully why we possibly sabotage our own success, why some of us choose to focus, in the most narcissistic of ways, exclusively on ourselves and how we can change the circumstances of our lives. As I have surveyed the landscape of human existence over the past twenty plus years of speaking, coaching, consulting and various other human interactions, my view is that most of us would like nothing better than the opportunity to change the circumstances of our lives in one form or another. This feeling is uniquely human and seems to bind most of us together, regardless of race, social standing, wealth or poverty.

I have adopted a consciousness that makes it possible for me to realize that life indeed is joyous at that moment when we have made the decision to take complete responsibility for all that we have become through the choices we have made.

Going forward, I will also introduce into your vernacular the concept of the *Hedonic Treadmill* that many of us are on in life. This term is not new. It was first introduced some thirty five years ago, and many psychology researchers have tweaked the theory over the years. The theory behind the Hedonic Treadmill is that our happiness stays in pretty much the same place regardless of what happens to us in life. It may move for a while if someone close to you dies, or if you win the lottery, but within a few months most people will return to their baseline level of happiness.

Understanding and accepting this theory will also help you to avoid becoming afflicted with one of life's greatest addictions: *Destination Addiction*, that never ending road of "If I just get this promotion, I will be happy; if I just make this amount of money or lose this amount of weight or do this amount of cosmetic surgery, I will be happy."

It's been said that formal education will make you a living, but that self-education will make you a fortune. That being said, I feel that personal self-discovery will unlock so many more than just the economic doors that may or may not have been closed for you in your walk through life.   I would suggest that greater awareness and understanding of others, appreciation for a full moon or the wonders of a rainy night much like the one that I am experiencing as I write this, are the kind of thoughts that move away from egocentric fulfillment of basic needs, money, power, dominance and lead you towards your legacy, your impact on the world. As you begin to emancipate yourself from mundane desires and to satiate your basic needs, you will then begin to illuminate your true purpose for living and to take the critical steps towards contributing to a cause that is greater than your own.

Your contribution finally has a name: *Self-actualization*. Self-actualization is the desire to realize one's full potential or to maximize one's capabilities; it is our instinctive human need to make the most of our abilities and to strive to be the best we can be. But what does this word mean? It means simply to reach and dwell in your fullest potential, to rise above ego-dominant thoughts of money, your position at work, etc. In essence, you transcend your fixation of meeting your basic needs for food, love, shelter, sex. Instead you now spend the majority of your time thinking at a higher level of consciousness. You are no longer self-absorbed; your higher consciousness gives rise to a higher form of living: a concern for those around you, your impact on them, and your ability to impact the world. Perhaps your thoughts and actions will move you toward feeding the hungry and otherwise helping those less fortunate than you. As we will explore further, these kinds of actions are the essence of a truly enlightened existential sage. I know some of you will say, "How am I to do this when I can barely feed my kids or take care of myself?" The same way I survived accidentally killing my best childhood friend at 17, the same way that I learned to accept my broken childhood along with many other tragedies in life.

You will have to make a conscious decision at a deep level, one that requires you to finally accept the circumstances of your youth, your pain in all its ugliness, and your actions as an adult, and to finally decide to make the necessary choices in your life that will enable you to manifest that which you desire.

But it goes even deeper. I have found that often people seem to have abundance in one area of their life. For example, they are wildly successful with their business and yet they seem to have disasters in their personal health or relationships. Or they may be wonderful parents and yet have little understanding of the real estate market or the financial issues which can result in dire consequences throughout their lifetimes.

This realization has led me to write a more comprehensive book, one that suggests if you make conscious decisions to be ignorant with your health or finances, you will be hard pressed to fully enjoy other parts of your life, and thus obtain a true sense of higher living.

Which is to say, if you enjoy a tremendous love in your life, for example, but your finances are a mess, these tend over time to blend together or come crashing together at some point, inhibiting you from truly becoming a fully functioning, creative person who can find your true purpose in your life. Finding your true purpose will be your way of jumping off the *Hedonic Treadmill* that most of us are on and beginning to enjoy life to its fullest potential. This is possible when people realize that achieving more material objects or possessions for example, will not bring them greater happiness. Higher living is on a micro level the difference between buying a six pack of soda or beer or buying a juicer knowing that a juicer will probably add many years to your life, along with making you feel better immediately. Since humans seek to avoid pain and pursue pleasure as much as possible, this would be a good start.

When the father of humanistic psychology Abraham Maslow stated: *What is necessary to change a person is to change his awareness of himself*, this simple and yet profound idea resonated with me so deeply that in essence it has become the hallmark of my reality and a guiding force in my becoming a self-actualizing human being. The more awareness that I developed within myself, the more I found that I could survive and overcome great tragedies and major setbacks. The longer we pursue this process of greater awareness, the less frequently we make mistakes and the better we seem to do in the business of "living life."

> *No problem can withstand the assault of sustained thinking*
>
> *-Voltaire*

Recently I watched an episode of the History channel that went into great detail on emerging technologies, including an electric battery operated car that can go from zero to sixty in under four seconds, travel distances of 200 miles with only a three hour charge time and reach a top speed of 130 mph.

Included in the show was a piece on a chemistry professor who had recently been awarded a U.S. Patent for the invention of nano-batteries. These batteries are so small that they can not be seen by the human eye and have to be put under an electron microscope. What disturbed me about this man was that his sheer brilliance in one area of his life earned him incredible accolades, and yet he was by my estimation almost 60 pounds overweight.

This professor suffers from a condition I have identified in people who have tremendous levels of intelligence and expertise in one area of life yet choose to completely ignore working on areas that, if improved, could save or pro-long their lives. I have coined a phrase to describe this con-dition: *Segment Deficiency.* In other words, he's completely mastered one part of his life while neglecting another, to the point that he may not survive past his mid-to-late 50s. He chooses not to use his higher form of education to reach a higher form of living.

This is not to say that we are not self-actualizing if all parts of our lives are not perfect. How could they be? Rather it is to say that when you choose a higher level of conscious-ness in the intellectual area – for example, obtaining your PhD – and yet you completely neglect other vital parts of your life, such as your health, how can you become bal-anced? To live a life with glaring segment deficiencies is not to be fully functioning, balanced, and on a path towards self-actualization, which means you are not becoming the best that you're capable of becoming.

Along my road that has been filled with so many set-backs, I have been fortunate to meet many people. Many of us face setbacks in life. We lose jobs, we go through divorce, we lose a loved one, we choose to be in very un-healthy and dysfunctional relationships, and we fill our bodies with needless addictions. What makes some of us turn massive roadblocks into giant success, while others seem to toil in their own mess, much of it self- inflicted? Many people live by a simple, misguided, and typically unconscious method. They fail to plan, therefore they plan to fail.

More than just failing to plan our lives we must also recognize that some of history's greatest thinkers have pos-tulated the existential belief that man is an absurd being run-ning loose in the universe, empty of any real meaning. This may strike you as a rather harsh way of looking at your exis-tence. As one who subscribes to existentialism, I truly believe that we are responsible for creating the meaning to our lives. Sadly though, myself included for many years, we as a people choose to vacillate from despair to joy, sometimes hour by hour in a rather neurotic state.

This state of consciousness reminds me of the power that we all have to take massive action to manifest a realty that we desire. This starts with finding ourselves and our voice. In his seminal work, *The Undiscovered Self*, author Dr. Carl Jung said it best when he stated, *"The suffocating power of the masses is paraded before our eyes in one form or another every day in the newspapers. The insignificance of the individual is rubbed into him so thoroughly that he loses all hope of making himself heard."* As I will espouse in the coming chapters, my hope is that you will come away from this book with a much louder voice and stronger conviction to achieve anything that you desire and to accelerate your life to the top floor of greatness. Quite a task, but one that is truly possible.

For example, the well-conditioned athlete who rises to the top of his or her profession benefits from something others do not have. Athletes have plans and coaches to help them reach their magnificent accomplishments.

A very successful businessman said the following to me as we discussed life and the road to success: "Glenn, in my life, I have a trainer come to my office three times a week so that I can stay fit and healthy, but most people get a trainer after a heart attack scare. I go to marriage counseling with my wife on a regular basis, so that we can continue to develop our relationship; most people seek out counseling as a last resort to save a relationship. I use a business coach to keep developing my company; most people seek out coaching when their business is failing."

The point of his story is that in those three important areas of his life, he was taking preventative, proactive steps to keep all aspects of his life moving forward, as opposed to most people who seek help only when they are in dire need.

To that end, my greatest inspiration for writing this book is you. So many people are going through difficult circumstances without a friend to lean on, wondering if other people have suffered as they are suffering, hoping to find answers to life's problems and the inspiration to overcome the obstacles that they face.

The following is my examination of the human condition, which at times you and I will both find to be quite disturbing. In the process I hope to coach you in the behavior, the attitudes, and the wisdom you need to help you unlock your greatest life. Is this the manual for living? For some it may be. In my view there is a dualism present in the human condition that resides in all of us. We will explore this further. My own survival dictated that I choose a life of self discovery, understanding this dualism and choosing to help others shift their consciousness. This mission became the greater purpose in my life.

This book will start with our exploration and detailed overview of human development and the basic needs to which we are all bound. These needs form the critical foundation on which rest our health, relationships, finances and purpose. In Part Two we will take a radical turn and focus on several examples of unconscious living, my own and others, and their devastating consequences. It has been my life's experience that true existential enlightenment comes from these types of major tragedies and much can be learned by exploring them. In Part Three we will shift our focus to your development of a prosperity consciousness. Much has been written about how to make money, save for retirement and so on, but in this section I will introduce one key example of how you could shift your consciousness about housing and chart a much different course for your life. I have chosen to make housing and credit a major focus of Part Three due to the fact that housing is not only one of our basic human needs but will also be one of your major primary assets in your lifetime. Given the fact that our country experiences significant cycles in the real estate sector and many people have little understanding of credit, this will be a primary vehicle for developing a greater awareness of your finances. In Part Four we will focus on health. Again, much has been already written in this area, and many of us understand what we need to do when it comes to eating well and exercising more. I will move you beyond the basics of health and focus on preventative health techniques that will require you to look inside of your body—something that many in our society ignore completely. By this point we will have addressed major areas of a person's life and can now focus in Part Five of the book on your path towards enlightenment and discovering your true purpose for living.

What follows is a detailed inventory of your life, covering your relationships, your finances, your body and health, your family, your friends and your career. This book is a call to action for you to master these five areas of life that we all have to deal with at some point if we are to achieve our ultimate success. I will walk you through the process and enable you to "clean house," helping you to define what it is that you truly want for your life and just as importantly, to develop a plan to get it. As a result, I hope you will gain much needed clarity on issues that have been of great challenge for you.

It is critical for you to understand that I wrote this book for you and about you. Many of my stories in Part Two of the book may give you the impression that this book is actually a memoir. On the contrary, I feel a good way to legitimize and reinforce my effort here is to provide examples from my own life. I hope that my stories, which are centered around the people in my life who have lived and died so very tragically, will be consumed by you, as they were by me, as great lessons and wisdom. For I see the people who leave us in death as the ultimate teachers.

Death commands center stage; it snaps us out of the egocentric me-me reality and shakes us to the core. It also teaches us, should we choose to accept these lessons. In looking back, death visited me early and often in life. As we explore these stories further, my hope is that it will resonate with you and move you toward higher forms of consciousness and awareness. In this process, I hope you will be well served and the ultimate benefactor. In short, this book is about you and your walk through life.

(It shall be noted that my use of the word "man" shall also be inclusive of women. It is my view that women are most certainly a man's equal and by no means do I wish to exclude them in my references. For the sake of style, flow and ease of absorption, I will make reference to man, but please take note that women are very much an equal part of that reference.)

Finally, I wrote this book in the hopes that it will take you from the deepest valleys in your life to your highest mountain. That it will inspire you to turn your company around, lose the weight that you have always wanted, or help you deal with overwhelming loss. That it will drive you to make changes in your relationships with others. Getting to that point in your business and or personal life can be a big task. Hopefully through this examination of the human condition and the many stories that unfold, you will discover a road map to radical change in your life. To that end I am reminded of Hemingway's great quote, "In order to write about life, first you must live it."

THE ENLIGHTENED EXISTENTIALIST

8 Points of Light.

As man's proclivity for unbridled, material accumulation, designed to satiate his ego, grows ever so large, one must adopt a referendum on such pursuits and engage his consciousness in a discourse that will ultimately lead towards the salvation of his soul. Rather than viewing life as a series of righteous indignations, he takes ultimate responsibility for his fate. As man finds a higher purpose he also becomes acutely aware of his eventual non-being. This realization in turn brings a sense of existential urgency to live our greatest life now.

There is a small stratum of man that flees from freedom and a life of higher living only to adopt a lower consciousness, thus becoming impregnated with a prolonged existential despair. Existentialism certainly could be summed up by Jean-Paul Sartre, the 20th century French existentialist philosopher and novelist, who simply stated: *"Man exists, encounters himself, surges up in the world and defines himself afterwords."* This partly explains man's existential existence, but I have wanted to explicate existential principles, as there are various forms of existential thought that have evolved over time. It is my view that these are the following tenants of existentialism that resonate within me and ultimately define me as an existentialist. Put another way, existentialism is concerned with the science of being, as an approach to living.

- Existentialism is an endeavor to grasp reality
- Existentialism is a philosophical movement which posits

that individuals create the meaning and essence of their lives, as opposed to deities or authorities creating it for them
■ We have freedom of choice; therefore people make decisions based upon what has meaning to them, rather than what is rational
■ Each of us must take responsibility for the consequences of our actions
■ Each of us must make our own way
■ We can and should become engaged, due to the absurdity of our existence, in a cause that is greater than our own
■ The universe offers more abundance and prosperity than people may realize, assuming that man desires to be authentic and true to his nature by pursuing his passions with his work
■ As an existentialist, it is imperative that you realize that you cannot complain about the things in your life that you are willing to condone

Boredom and anxiety are the two hallmarks of human existence that differentiate us from all other animals. The fact that humans have a past, present and future consciousness enables us to eradicate the many possibilities that exist for our lives. Enter Rollo May and his seminal work, *The Discovery of Being*, which resonates with me deeply. He gives us clarity to existential thinking when he states: *"The existentialists do not mean "distant future" or anything connected with using the future as an escape from the past or present. They mean only to indicate that the human being, so long as he possesses self-awareness and is not incapacitated by anxiety or neurotic rigidities, is always in a dynamic self-actualizing process, always exploring, molding himself and moving into the immediate future."*

Certainly their have been many times in my own life where I was completely imprisoned in a state of fear and anxiety; fear of how I was going to pay the rent, how I was going to find a better job and so on. Once we let this fear go, we empower ourselves to make forward progress in our lives. Letting go of fear and anxiety in my view becomes a conscious choice. As we will explore further throughout the coming chapters, this is not only possible but incredibly liberating. It has only been within the past few years of my walk through life that I have been able to accomplish this task. As a crescendo of self-awareness took hold of me and my ability and desire to finally acknowledge the suffering of others, came to an apex, I was finally free of these toxic states of being. If you take nothing else from this book, understanding and truly embracing this paradigm shift that took place within me and most certainly can take place within you, will be one of the most significant gifts to yourself that one could ever hope for.

MODERN MAN'S AFFLICTION WITH DUALISM

Over 6,000 years of history has been recorded prior to your showing up on earth. Desire to set sail on your own journey, on a voyage of discovery, exploring the world's great knowledge and wisdom. This is a process that will provide you with an ocean of prosperity and abundance.

Glenn Gary

There is a dualism present within the human condition that is running loose in your consciousness and resides in all of us. Once you begin to vibrate at this higher level of awareness, anything in your life becomes possible. If you were to look up the definition of dualism you would find that it is defined as "a doctrine that the universe is under the dominion of two opposing principles one of which is good and the other evil." Another definition would be that human beings posses "the quality or state of being dual or of having a dual nature." For example, the Yin and Yang symbolizes the duality in nature. In the philosophy of mind, dualism is a set of views about the relationship between mind and matter. Aristotle dealt with speculations as to the existence of an incorporeal soul which bares the faculties of intelligence and wisdom. There are many other ways that dualism is used and perceived throughout the history of time. In my view, modern man becomes dualistic at that moment that he is confronted with an assault on his true nature. In our modern world, the over-crowded, bloated masses of concrete that we call freeways are unique places that bring our duality to a fluid, sudden and potentially life threatening crescendo. For example, on numerous occasions I have been driving along with the feeling that I am truly an instrument of peace, enjoying my music and thinking of what I will do when I arrive at my destination. Suddenly, and without warning, some unevolved madman from hell screams by my car at 100 mph and decides to cut in front of me. At that very moment, my body races with rage and I morph into a smaller version of the Incredible Hulk. Pure, unadulterated rage and venom are the only things that have captured my soul at that moment. I could go on but the point is many of us have experienced this incredible road rage and we have reacted in various ways and to various degrees. Our duality oftentimes only needs to be provoked for it to rear it's ugly head.

It becomes clear to me that we have to decide in our minds two things as we walk through life. For example, a woman of Christian faith said to me several years ago, "Glenn, I believe that we are in hell, that life on earth is hell and only when we die, will we go to a better place." How you see reality and your response to reality will dictate the outcome and quality of your life. If you perceive reality as if everyone around you is out to get you and so on, then you may have a very hard time with your journey through life. The other reality, as I have outlined in the scenario above, would suggest that man certainly has a proclivity to act upon his evil desires when provoked or threatened; however man does have a choice. For example, my own personal growth now mandates that I respond in a positive way when confronted with one of these dualistic quagmires. Back in 1867, chances are cars were not screaming by you on a freeway, but you would have had men everywhere with guns, ready to take your life, quite possibly for doing nothing more than looking at them the wrong way. The point is, modern man is subjected to many threats. Understanding your dualistic nature and making a conscious decision for self-preservation by not responding to evil with evil embodies the growth within you; this growth is one that takes place on your path towards greater awareness. True enlightenment comes from understanding that many people around you suffer from unevolved thinking and a lack of greater awareness. As a result they respond to their own pent up frustration, lack of achievement, feelings of inadequacy, repressed desires and envy by behaving in various nonsensical ways.

Another situation that exemplifies the above is when people driving horrible looking cars drive by your nice car and cutt you off. Drive a freeway for an hour or two and notice how people respond to each other. It becomes a fascinating glimpse into the reality of modern man. It has taken me many years to disengage from responding to this in a negative fashion. Think of your own driving as a manifestation of how you feel. You will see that if you are angry, impatient and frustrated with the direction of your life, you may tend to drive like a complete idiot. The rubric that man lives by suddenly becomes suspended as he seeks to cavil at his dualistic nature. At this moment his life and the many lives of other people are on the line. Lest you think that I am espousing about something that does not come into play in our lives, think about the fact that almost everyday, somewhere in America, you and I jump on a freeway. This freeway in my view is not a corridor of transportation. Rather it has become the stage for all of us to manifest where our minds are functioning in relation to our higher consciousness or lack thereof.

The hieroglyphic writing is on the wall, but many of us can't seem to figure it out. Modern man's plight with his dualistic nature, to respond either with love or with hate to any situation, is encapsulated in the timeless message of Dr.

Martin Luther King, lest we forget his soulful words (previously quoted): "...*the ultimate test of a man is not where he stands in moments of comfort and moments of convenience, but where he stands in moments of challenge and moments of controversy.*" I echo these sentiments as I am fully aware of the duality of our nature. This awareness becomes the critical first step at doing something to control it and this can lead to a life saving way of dealing with the threats of modern times.

Part 1

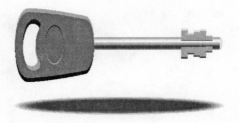

Basic Human Development
& Needs

6 Stages To Living Your Greatest Life

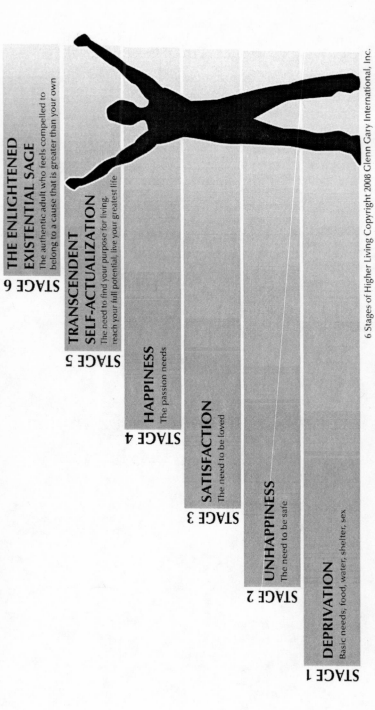

STAGE 6

THE ENLIGHTENED EXISTENTIAL SAGE
The authentic adult who feels compelled to belong to a cause that is greater than your own

STAGE 5

TRANSCENDENT SELF-ACTUALIZATION
The need to find your purpose for living, reach your full potential, live your greatest life

STAGE 4

HAPPINESS
The passion needs

STAGE 3

SATISFACTION
The need to be loved

STAGE 2

UNHAPPINESS
The need to be safe

STAGE 1

DEPRIVATION
Basic needs; food, water, shelter, sex

UNDERSTANDING THE SIX LEVELS OF HUMAN DEVELOPMENT

I knew that if I allowed all the bitter setbacks and tragedies, disappointments and neglect in my life to engulf me, I would self-destruct with anger, hatred and rage. Self-discovery and working through these feelings was the only way for me to come out the other side and find a bright light in the darkness that was my life. I had a choice: I could wallow in my own misery about the circumstances and events of my life, or I could choose to build a cathedral of abundance from the ashes that was my past.

Glenn Gary

I have been fascinated for many years now by the different levels of consciousness that people from all walks of life come to inhabit. As I discuss these levels or stages, I do not mean to suggest that a person is somehow inferior due to the fact that they operate at a lower level of conscious thought. Nor do I mean to suggest that I am at a higher level, and therefore I must be a better person. Quite to the contrary: if we are to reach higher levels of success in our health, our relationships, and our business, we will have to take the time to understand, at a deeper level, where we are and where our friends, family and business contacts are.

In my view, our ability to understand these levels of human development will help us to create the reality that we seek. As I have previously mentioned, awareness of these levels is nothing new to the small percentage of our society that has studied these issues. Critical thinkers, including Dr. M. Scott Peck, in his best selling book, *The Road Less Traveled,* have postulated that four stages of human spiritual development exist. Though I credit his work with influencing part of my thinking, over many years I experienced more stages that enabled me to expand upon his framework. The Psychology of Higher Living is presented to you in order for you to adopt radical, authentic changes that will last a lifetime. Sadly and regrettably, I find the ending of Peck's life to resemble the tragic dimensions of the human condition that some choose to adopt. In summarizing his life, biographers noted the following during an interview from the last year of his life:

"He spent much of his life as an alcoholic immersed in cheap gin, chain-smoking cigarettes and inhaling cannabis. Now, since pancreatitis has stopped his drinking, he still chain smokes, however, and it is a little pitiful watching the difficulty he has working his lighter in the breeze."

Though I do not relish or desire to be disparaging of Peck or his significant accomplishments and contributions, he clearly deviated from the road less traveled and went down the one that many choose. This left a profound impact on me and further cemented my theory that I submit to you. Through my own experiences and research I clearly have discovered six stages of human development. Going forward, I only hope to present my findings in a more evolved form based on my own walk with adversity, tragedy and success in life.

Stage I consciousness is chaotic, disordered, and reckless. Very young children are in Stage I. They tend to defy and disobey, unwilling to accept a will greater than their own. Many criminals are people who have never grown out of Stage I. I would suggest that many adults are operating in stage one, evidenced by their very chaotic and dysfunctional relationships, where they tend to feast on consistent forms of daily chaos. If they are not creating or dealing with some form of chaos, they do not feel comfortable. This may not be something they are willing to admit or be aware of, but somehow these people always seem to need to be in conflict with other people, often those with whom they are romantically involved.

From first hand experience I can tell you that living with someone who seeks a consistent level of conflict and chaos is like riding a roller coaster from hell. If you have found yourself attached to someone who operates at this level of consciousness, you may be finding it very hard to walk away, but in the end I would suggest that your salvation lies in doing so. Many adults operate at this low level, however, and they may be some of the most charismatic and attractive people you have ever laid eyes on.

Stage II is the stage in which a person has blind faith. Once children learn to obey their parents, they reach Stage II. Many so-called religious fanatics who are members of cults are essentially Stage II people, in the sense that they have blind faith in a supreme being and do not question its existence. With blind faith comes humility and a willingness to obey and serve. Operating from this vantage point in life has its downside. Never questioning conventional knowledge can be a form of self-induced ignorance.

Such blind faith can lead people to judge and even condemn others for their beliefs, which can lead to fractured families. I should know; for many years my mother's side of the family has operated from a very specific religious faith that dictated that if you did not subscribe to their beliefs, your one way-ticket to hell was all but guaranteed. This is a very uncompassionate way of viewing your fellow man or woman.

To that end, I do not feel that you will enjoy peace in your life if you unconsciously operate at Stage II; it will become a defining line in the sand that many others will not want to cross. It will also serve to alienate you from people who could enrich your life. For example, recently in my own family, I felt this alienation when one member could not appreciate the great wisdoms of the Tao Te Ching that I was attempting to share. My family member decided that she felt I was trying to somehow supersede the teachings of the Bible and therefore would have no part of it. Such rigid adherence to her own faith has prevented her from enjoying other wisdoms. The Bible is a wonderful source of spiritual enlightenment and guidance, but not the only place that encapsulates great teachings and wisdoms.

Stage III is the stage of skepticism and curiosity. A Stage III person does not accept things on blind faith but only accepts them if *convinced* logically. Many people working in scientific and technological research are in Stage III. I would suggest that these Stage III people are critical for the survival of mankind as we know it.

The highly evolved forms of thinking that lead a Stage III person to question all things and accept nothing on blind faith are the foundation for great discoveries in the world. I also feel that in your own life, the more you can question aspects of your life, the assumptions and motives of your co-workers, friends and family, and the conventional beliefs of your society, without obsessively overanalyzing (something omnipresent in my family), the more likely you are to make better decisions and choices.

It will also help you to determine who and what should be in your life, and even more importantly, why you do what you do. If for example, you are entirely consumed with thoughts of material achievements, you will find your path to be a lonely one characterized by a never-ending need to acquire.

Your careful examination of all parts of your life, from the ingredients of food you eat to the people that you allow into your life and the information that you choose to take in and adopt, will be the critical, determining factor in the levels of success that you attain. Success in not an accident; it is the clever pursuit of a goal by a person who is committed to reaching it. However, many of us know people who are quite successful in business, but severely deficient in other parts of their life.

This dichotomy is present in many people. I would submit that a Stage III person is operating at a high enough consciousness to see these glaring segment deficiencies in his or her life and to seek more balance. This may be in the form of accepting only healthy relationships into your life, or recognizing that you can survive a divorce, or realizing that all the money in the world won't make you happy or save you if you neglect your health.

Stage IV this is where an individual chooses to speak with more compassion or show greater empathy for others around them, disconnecting from actions emanating from egocentric behavior, and instead beginning the search for more meaning and purpose to their lives. It is also at this critical stage that people recognize the anger and hate that may have imprisoned them and they are able to begin the steps of letting go of these harmful and negative emotions. There became a very defining point in my own life where I was able to let go of intense anger towards my father. This was something that I never thought I could do, but I realized that once I did, I was now free to use my considerable energy in more important aspects of my life. Many of us carry around deep resentments towards the people in our lives that have hurt us. Your ability to free yourself from this toxic and crippling emotion will be a liberating experience. We see examples of anger in our society on a daily basis. For example, most of us know that we occasionally suffer from temporary bouts of road rage as we drive down a crowded freeway. In moments like these, a Stage IV person would strive to transcend these negative temptations to lash out at fellow drivers and search within him or herself for a greater sense of peace. People who cut you off and drive poorly are most likely feeling pretty crummy about their lives and are attempting to find empowerment by bullying you at 70 mph.

Stage IV people recognize that hanging onto justified resentments only weakens them. It is also at this stage that people turn away from their own egocentric views of the world and learn to enjoy the mystery and beauty of nature. When drama and chaos cease to exist and your walk through life becomes more purposeful, you will notice even the smallest forms of nature that you may have either taken for granted or missed altogether with your previous lack of awareness. A Stage IV person's religion and spirituality differ significantly from that of a Stage II person in the sense that he/she does not accept things through blind faith but through genuine belief.

Stage IV people tend to be more independent, self motivated, and possibly entrepreneurial, and at the very least don't subscribe to workplace bullying or politics. Rather than engage in wasteful pursuits of high school shenanigans that often engulf many of our corporate environments, they will tend to be thinking about higher forms of personal self-development and their impact on the world. Stage IV people are often labeled as mystics.

Whether you see yourself as a mystic is up to you. I would however suggest that it is at Stage IV that we begin to really arrive and more importantly strive for higher forms of thought which will lead to finding our purpose.

Stage V is a stage at which people start to complete the process of self- actualization. This is to say they recognize where their full potential has not been met and they seek to reach it. They set out a clear plan as to what their purpose for living is and they go to work on that plan. They begin to recognize that life is not just about the fancy house, the Mercedes or BMW in the driveway, the promotion or power grab at work, or the famous and well-connected friends they may have. They also recognize that any sudden, newfound emergent materialism in their lives is taken with a humble gratefulness. Nothing shows the arrogance of an individual more than someone who gains a sudden new found level of prosperity, only to feel the overwhelming need to propagate this for all of us to see. The true nature of a person is often exposed when sudden abundance and prosperity take hold. We saw quite a bit of this over the past few years prior to the housing crash. For example, many people involved in real estate or mortgage banking were awash with abundance, only to see this vaporize within a few short years. Many handled this newfound prosperity with grace, while others did so with excessive, egocentric, over indulgent flamboyance. Stage V people are in the process of understanding that their ego-driven consumption is not sustainable in a world crying out for people to operate at higher levels. Maybe they decide to build a well in Africa for a few thousand dollars or feed the hungry or less fortunate in their city. Maybe it's not about money at all but about the legacy that they leave behind.

In Stage V, your life is no longer a sophisticated game of monopoly. Instead you seek greater meaning to your life found in who you help and how you contribute to the world. You seek to escape the Hedonic Treadmill and no longer are afflicted with Destination Addiction; rather you understand that life is a process, a never ending series of chapters that you will write. Happiness is not the end result, but the way.

That is to say that you have accepted all that you have and all that you have not achieved. You send blame for your lot in life away, and you adopt acceptance. You understand that life is a complicated series of interactions with many people, all who operate at different levels. In Stage IV you may have started to ask yourself, what your purpose is. In Stage V you have taken massive action towards that purpose. There is a clear distinction between Stage IV and V. Stage IV is where we begin our search for higher levels of awareness. We start to identify that we need a greater meaning to our lives and a greater purpose. By Stage V you have fully committed to that purpose and are living each day towards leaving a footprint of your life behind. You will start to develop an overwhelming desire to self-actualize, to achieve all that you are capable of, regardless of the risks. Your purpose becomes a center stage from which you operate. Getting up to trudge to work just to make a buck no longer works for you.

Maybe you have operated a successful law practice for twenty plus years, much like a gentleman that I recently met, and you have "been there done that" but yet are not fulfilled. Maybe the law was originally where you thought your passion and talent lay, but after twenty years, you no longer feel that you are on purpose. Stage V people ask themselves these hard questions. They have a need to disconnect from their egos and connect with others at a deeper level.

They also want to explore their purpose. Maybe it's writing that great novel, starting a new career or buying a new business. Maybe it's living in Europe and traveling the world to do some form of good. Maybe it's slowing down and recognizing that every day there is a beautiful sky, an ocean and nature all around us, and yet we get so consumed by jumping in our cars and trudging to the office, fighting traffic and possibly our co-workers, and in the process, watch life passing us by.

Stage V people start to hunger for connections to the environment, for living and feeling life at higher levels. They tend to successfully avoid negative dysfunctional relationships that don't enhance their life, and they are highly aware that if they ignore their health, they may not live past the age of 50.

Even in the most trivial moments in life, the Stage V person will continue to show respect for others. For example, they are people that are more apt to return your phone calls or emails instead of blowing you off. They understand the eternal struggle that we all go through in order to make a living, but because they operate from a center of greater compassion and empathy for people, they will simply show you that respect rather then to ignore you or hide from you. Stage V people have a greater need for independence, which may manifest itself in the work that they choose, and they strive to avoid dependence on their fellow man or woman. This independence rather than co-dependence enables them to seek higher levels of conscious thought.

Stage V people tend to not engage in hero or celebrity worship for the simple fact that all of God's children have been created equal. To be focused on the firestorm that is Britney Spears or fascinated by Paris Hilton only takes away from your own life. Those among us seeking to operate at higher levels of consciousness would never waste time in watching other people live their greatest life; we are much too busy contributing to others and our own life to pay close attention to those labeled "celebrity."

Stage V people desire to connect with their loved ones at a deeper level, realizing that by doing so, they transcend their egocentric desires and gain a much greater sense of purpose and joy. For example, the dog no longer becomes an inferior being that you feel comfortable leaving outside in the cold; rather he is an extension of your own humanity. It's my personal view that people who merely own pets and are incapable of showering them with love are truly void of love for themselves.

Stage VI is where a person occupies that rarified air of the enlightened existential sage; that is, the authentic adult who is beyond ego and self-actualizing. This person, who accepts his or her possible non-being, faces this anxiety with the courage to acknowledge the tremendous suffering that exists in the world. It is a time when a person's cumulated wisdom collides with their desire to become fully engaged in a cause that is greater than their own, one that saves and or impacts lives directly. Here is where we see that Stage V people have clearly defined a purpose that allows them to reach their own full potential, whether this be losing significant weight, removing negative relationships from their lives or having the courage to pursue their dreams and start a business. These are all things that directly benefit the individual. It is at Stage VI that we seek to directly benefit and become involved in a cause that is greater than our own. Having fulfilled our needs, we are now free to focus our attention on others. It is my firm belief that a person who sacrifices their own prosperity and abundance is much less capable of helping others. We are on this earth to be happy, healthy, wealthy and wise. It is critical that we experience life to its fullest potential. Cutting yourself short of these attainments does not empower you to help others. A healthy, rich, prosperous and joyful person can unleash much more power and resources to causes in the world that desperately need your help. Let's be clear here, your sending a check to your local charity for $20,000 is great. However, I am espousing that you getting on a plane, with $20,000 in your pocket and flying to Africa so that you can directly participate in the saving of lives, is more of what I am referring to here. Stage VI people do not approach these activities with ambivalence, but rather with a sustained vigilance that intoxicates others around them to also become involved. This would not include the morally bankrupt, unevolved and utterly barbaric human that feels the need to go big-game hunting in Africa. Your walk on the enlightened path of human existence would preclude you from feeling the need to kill animals as if it were some sort of sport. A Stage VI person seeks to operate at altruistic levels at all times. Anything short of this becomes a vacant way to live for this individual. It is my view that living life in an eloquent fashion mandates that you truncate your egocentric impulses and adopt a greater awareness of the fact that you can save lives.

9 Basic Needs
Form The Foundation For Our Lives

9. The need to belong to a cause greater than your own

8. The need to self-actualize

7. The passion needs

6. The need for self expression

5. The need for the EGO to dominate

4. The esteem needs

3. The need to be loved

2. The need for security and safety

1. The basic physiological needs: food, water, shelter, sleep, sex

CHANGING YOUR LIFE BY UNDERSTANDING THE 9 BASIC HUMAN NEEDS

I submit that luck does not exist; rather luck happens when an opportunity arises for which we are prepared, and we lead it to success.

Glenn Gary

Some time ago, I became interested in learning how psychologists forty-five years ago first started to define our basic needs and to put them into a hierarchy. Specifically, Abraham Maslow is credited with defining the five basic needs.

I have gone several steps further and identified four other critical needs that play a dominant role in our daily lives and overall development. I suggest then there are nine areas of needs to be met if we are to become fully self-actualized, enlightened existential sages. In my view, Maslow was a groundbreaking, wonderful man who gave the world a definitive understanding of needs and how they relate to our daily behavior. Over the preceding decades his hierarchy of needs has become prevalent in our consciousness. But like many concepts that we can look back on that were developed fifty years ago, I suggest that he may have overlooked some important additional needs that in my view are important to articulate. Modern man has been in need of an updated understanding of these critical areas. Since I did not have the honor or pleasure to know Maslow, I can only speculate that he may not have had the opportunity to live and experience these other needs or perhaps he just did not pay them the attention that I feel they so desperately deserve. It is also clear that a part of our society is not even fully conscious enough to even be able to identify these needs that may lay dormant somewhere in their unevolved minds. For example, I am referring to criminals or to unevolved neanderthal drivers that feel the need to cut you off on the freeway while speeding by you at 90 mph, endangering your life and many others. The list would not be complete without my favorite group of unconscious adults --- the hunters, people who feel the need to kill beautiful animals in order to satiate their barbaric need for dominance.

What I will be presenting to you is the problematic process most of us go through in attempting to satiate these basic needs, a process that involves intense pressure and yet traps us into concentrating only on lower level needs. This process prevents you from finding your true purpose in life and thus from reaching the states of higher living that most of us desire.

Researchers have been clear to tell us that human needs arrange themselves in hierarchies of importance. The appearance of one need usually rests on the prior satisfaction of another, more important need. Men and women are perpetually needing something. It is also clear that no need or drive can be treated as if it were isolated or discrete; every drive is related to the state of satisfaction or dissatisfaction of other drives.

1) The physiological needs: Food, Water, Sleep, and Sex

The "food" needs include the need for proteins, sugar, and in my case, lots of caffeine from Starbucks. All joking aside, this is a conscious, daily decision on my part. Judging by the millions of cups of coffee that Starbucks sells every morning in America, it's safe to say that coffee has become a basic need for many people.

Another basic need for people is to avoid pain, something that many people spend inordinate amounts of time trying to do throughout their lives. Most people spend most of their time on these basic needs. I myself have also been trapped in this bewildering state in which I look back over my whole day and see that nothing was accomplished except meeting these basic needs. These can also be categorized as deprivation needs or deficit needs. If any one of these basic needs becomes a deficit in your life, look out, because this is where most of your time will be spent.

Obviously if we are hungry, we cannot focus on work; if we are thirsty or lacking sleep or money, we humans focus like laser beams on meeting these basic needs. Sadly, millions of Americans never move beyond these deficit needs and spend the majority of their time trying to satiate them. Though money can not be categorized as a basic human need, it certainly ties in with providing the means to satiating our basic needs.

2) The need for security and safety

Once basic needs have been met, most people start to think about how secure they are. This can manifest itself in many areas, from job security to financial security to physical or home security. For decades in this country, insurance companies have done well because they fulfill people's security needs by selling insurance. Adults tend to give way to fear and anxiety when these security and safety needs are not met, sometimes going into a tailspin, a physical and emotional response to circumstances.

Having studied and researched the way these issues affect people, I have come to learn that a vast majority get so consumed with level one and two needs that health takes a back seat, which may lead to a person's premature downfall. My father is one such example. For many years he was a couch potato, working from 8 to 4, coming home, grabbing something to eat, and taking his place in front of the TV, only to repeat this routine all over again the next day, never pushing himself to higher living or taking risks to achieve his life goals and thus failing to become fully self-actualized. Escaping this desperate trap is critical, and yet millions of people fall into this routine.

3) The need to be loved

Ever wonder why we have a gang problem in the United States that is reaching dangerous and epic proportions? Look no further than this third level need, the need for belonging. Certainly this does not entirely explain the gang problem, but it is a major contributing factor in our society. If you find yourself or your friends always "needing" to be in a relationship or always choosing the wrong person, unable to be alone for more than an evening, level three needs of love are usually at the root of it. Most healthy people want to be loved.

Once again though, your levels of greater awareness and higher consciousness will dictate whether you arrive at the relationship in a healthy state. Once we have taken care of basic physical needs and safety needs, we free our minds, and what naturally begins to come into our consciousness is the yearning for romance or some sort of physical connection with another person, which explains why millions of people get married.

In addition many people begin to climb onto the *Hedonic Treadmill* in their lives, which only leads one to *Destination Addiction*: the feeling that if I just achieve this goal or attract this awesome person into my life, all will be well. If I just get that job promotion or make more than $300,000 this year, my life will be great.

Nothing could be further from the truth. Promotions, money and wonderful people in our lives definitely make a big impact, but it is how you feel inside and your own love, self-respect and feelings of self-worth that will sustain these temporary feelings of joy and turn them into something that is much more powerful, a sustained sense of joy as you begin to identify your true purpose and go about living that purpose. Promotions, money and people in your life are ultimately temporary.

4) The esteem needs

After our belonging needs and or love needs are met, we set our sights on self-esteem needs. This also embodies the need to be respected by others; in corporate America and boardrooms everywhere, we see the self-esteem need being met by the status that we seek. In the entertainment industry we see the need manifest itself as a desire for fame. In professional sports it comes in the form of the need for glory, recognition. In boxing, for example, it's the need to utterly dominate your opponent.

A higher form is one in which we seek greater levels of self-respect; we want to be able to feel confident, to feel we have achieved something of significance in our lives. As a small example of this, each week I display this need on the tennis court, where I play on a competitive ladder with some forty other players, partly because trying to serve a tennis ball at speeds of over 100 mph is a lot of fun, but I also want to walk off that court feeling confident that I achieved something. It has been said that we crave the respect of others, yet once we have our own self-respect, we can hang onto it much more easily than we hang on to the respect that comes and goes from the people around us. Certainly when we compete against others, whether it be a game of tennis or possibly you're a teacher and striving to have your class achieve higher scores, we are attempting to meet our own self-esteem needs and gain the respect from others that are around us. On the flip side, when we suffer from low self-esteem, we tend to get into very dysfunctional relationships. Self-esteem needs can often work in conjunction with our egos.

5) The need for the ego to dominate

The inability to suspend our ego or our own self importance stands in the way of any further development, for we are held hostage to our egos, and only through a greater awareness will we even be conscious of how destructive a role the ego and its dominance can play in our lives. At many levels of human activity, from the work environment to friendships to our romantic connections, the ego is a dominant central figure in these activities and prevents us from achieving higher degrees of success in these areas.

The feeding of the ego with more stuff, with nicer cars, with more expensive homes and toys can become pervasive and take center stage in our life. Much of our spending can be traced to the feeding of the ego. It is a natural instinct for the ego to dominate our actions and social relationships. I submit that egocentric behavior serves to alienate people. It must be a conscious decision on our part to understand that the feeding of our ego can also serve as a force of destruction in our life. Though it may be natural for our ego to dominate, I suggest that we will need to acknowledge this and develop the ability to suspend our ego as we start to move towards higher forms of living and higher levels of consciousness and hopefully embark on new missions to connect with and serve the needs of others, whether it be opening a child care facility or donating time to a charity or becoming involved in a cause greater than your own.

6) The need for self-expression

All of us at some point in our lives have had an overwhelming need for self-expression. One could argue that writing this book is my attempt to satiate my need for self-expression. Of course I would argue back that I have an even higher need, and that is to help people. Self-expression is seen everywhere, from people who get tattoos to express their own uniqueness and separate themselves from society, to those who spend the day detailing their car so that he or she can display to the world their passion. It is in the artist who feels compelled to paint, the speaker to speak, the writer to write, the dancer to dance, the florist to display flowers, and the winemaker to make wine. "As a pet owner, my self-expression manifests itself by taking my dog Bosco for a walk." For every struggling artist, guitarist, singer and drummer there is a need to express talent in the form of music. Self-expression is everywhere at almost every time. It is the one thing that makes us unique. Sadly, when this need becomes dominant and collides with feelings of inadequacy, our self-expression reaches epic proportions and can wreak havoc in our lives. For example, in the out-of-control teenager feeling the need to express himself and achieve a sense of power in a drag race, only to crash and kill those around him, this reckless self-expression is deadly. In the corporate world we see CEOs and presidents become aloof and removed from the rest of the company, yet their need to express their power and control can have devastating consequences. For many women it may be the need to become mothers. For others, it may be plastic surgery. All of us are involved in some form of self-expression. The question that must be asked if we are to seek a state of higher living is the following: "is this form of self-expression a healthy one, or one that puts me or others in danger?"

7) The passion needs

Where my thinking differs from the original architect of the hierarchy of basic needs is in our need for passion. I believe that in order to fully self-actualize, you must first have one or more passions in your life that will help to propel you forward. I submit that this, our seventh basic need, precedes the need to self-actualize. For example, a passion for owning a business that leads to great financial success serves to fulfill many of the basic need levels and also provides the financial resources to focus your attention on higher forms of living. A passion for someone who brings great stability, love, affection and support into your life will liberate you in other areas of your life, freeing you to focus your attention and spend your time at a higher level. Many people that I coach have a passion deficit in their life as it relates to their careers and relationships, and sadly, many people have not spent the time to identify a passion that could possibly be translated to their work.

For some, passion can be defined as that special moment when you are kissing someone new for the first time, and you feel so alive. After years of being in a relationship where passion was non-existent, where kissing someone was no longer fun or even practiced, where anger and bitter resentment dominated, the sudden experience of passion can be the vital fuel that makes us feel alive again. Maybe it's a first or second date with someone that really ignites us; maybe it's finding a purpose in a new career. A life without this kind of passion can never illuminate your soul and lift you; instead you will be bitter and unhappy. Many people that I coach have described a life where passion ceases to be a part of their existence altogether, and they yearn for this intoxicating fuel.

Passion comes in all forms and in many activities. For me, it's my weekly battle to climb up a tennis ladder and see if I can become the best. I have a huge passion for this game. At some points during the year, I find myself utterly disgusted or frustrated with the game, so I simply pull back until I have begun to miss it and find new passion for it. Additionally, during several years in my late twenties and early thirties, I developed a huge passion for Latin dance-sport, like the mambo, and the cha cha, or as many have come to know it, ballroom dancing. My point is it is absolutely critical that you find a passion for something. In doing so you bring new meaning to your life. I could write a book on my love for dogs, and I know one day it will lead me to owning a shelter or some kind of rescue facility. My love for dogs is immense.

My passion for speaking and writing has led me to you here today, and yet I have coached many people who seem to be void of passion in their lives, stuck in unfulfilling jobs or relationships. A self-imposed exile in these areas leaves people with feelings of disgust, unhappiness and worthlessness.

The feelings that a person may have for someone who mistreats them, takes them for granted, and so on is not passion. That feeling is in fact codependency and is characterized by their inability to be free of that person's hold on them. If we have passion in one area of our lives then we can use that to build other areas and begin the process of constructing the life that we want, one that works and has meaning. For many, the concept that we could actually make money while pursuing a passion is a radical and inconceivable one. But that type of negative, self-limiting thinking is what keeps many people at level one consciousness. We can make unlimited amounts of money by following a passion, but in the end what matters is how much we desire to seek the higher levels of consciousness that will help us to find, explore, and pursue these passions.

All of us can find and become passionate about several things in our lives. I submit that this is absolutely vital to our evolving to higher levels and towards eventual self-actualization.

8) The need to self-actualize

As we develop as mature adults, we tend to move through these needs. You can recognize this in your kids as you observe them evolve from the need for food, water, and sleep to a sense of belonging and love and so on. During my own walk in life I have recognized many times where an overwhelming, reality-shaking situation has caused me to regress and look to simply meet my lower needs. The human condition naturally makes us focus on what we don't have; for example, when we lose a job we can't seem to stop thinking about or worrying about money. If we have a good career but are lonely most of the time, love, attention or affection seems to dominate our thoughts. For some, not enough satisfaction with themselves makes them yearn to gossip and rip others apart. The challenge is to break these cycles. Many who have suffered severe neglect or abuse as children or who faced prolonged periods of neglect tend to spend inordinate amounts of time "seeking" something as adults that was missing in their lives as children.

The U. S. Army some years ago spent tens of millions of dollars on the ad slogan, "Be all that you can be." It was a message that resonated with millions of young Americans for many years, but it also is a simplistic way of trying to define what it means to be engaged in self-actualization, in fulfilling your potential, in becoming a person that leaves a footprint on society, where generations will know that you have lived. A self-actualized person lives life on his or her own terms, transcending ego and basic needs and moving on to higher living, transcending dead end jobs, dead end relationships, poor health and so on. This person does not have segment deficiencies in his or her life. I have often felt in my own life experiences that if I want to be truly self-actualizing, I need to have my lower needs taken care of, at least to a considerable extent. As we study these nine basic needs the following question arises. When our lower needs are unmet, where will we find the time to devote ourselves to fulfilling our potential, to discovering our purpose? My own life experiences have led me to answer that it is critical that we understand and meet these needs so that we may focus on developing our true purpose for living.

9) The need to belong to a cause that is greater than your own

That true purpose for living can manifest itself in our need to belong to a cause that is greater than our own. This to me is where we inhabit the illustrious and rarified space in life where we finally stop focusing on our own selfish interests and begin the enlightening experience of helping others. Make no mistake; this is a watershed moment in our lives. This is also in one way very difficult for many people to grasp. In other ways, once you have expanded your world view and reinvented your thinking, you'll ask yourself why the hell it took you so long to get here! I know I did. Letting go of egocentric and narcissistic me-me type of self-centered consciousness is liberating and powerful. **In my view it is**

the manifesto of the enlightened existential sage. A person of great wisdom is one who sees beyond his own needs and works to satiate them. Once he develops his own abundance and prosperity he is then free to unleash the full zenith of his considerable talents and resources towards affecting the lives of others. Saving lives will pay huge dividends when you look back over the landscape of your own life. Rather than feeling much regret as many often do, you can tally the number of people you helped along the way, possibly the thousands of lives that you have saved, and the world will finally know that you have lived. Your legacy will leave a lasting footprint in the sands of time. Is there any way one could live that could be more magnificent? *I hardly think so.*

BREAKING THE CYCLE: FINDING YOUR TRUE PURPOSE

L et's break down a typical day in the life of the average American. You sleep for 7 hours, it takes another hour to get ready for work, and it takes the average person one hour to drive to work, assuming a typical 8-5 workday. With another hour drive home, you have 19 hours used so far.

Monday through Friday:

11pm to 6am sleep

6-7am get ready for work

7-8 drive to work

8am to 5pm work

5pm to 6pm drive home

6:00 to 8:00 eat

8pm to 9pm, collapse, relax, get your second wind, play with kids etc

9-10pm, couple time? TV?

10pm, hit the bed

Saturday: Sleep in, clean the house, wash the cars, take the kids to soccer etc.

Sunday morning: Sleep in, possibly attend church, etc.

Looking at this schedule more closely, we see that the typical person addresses basic needs for sleep, for money and for food for the vast majority of the week. This schedule explains why it is estimated that only 2 to 4 percent of Americans achieve self-actualization, in which they reach their full potential, for example becoming financially independent and thus freeing up time to discover their true purpose in life. The majority of a person's week is spent on basic needs, which explains how important it is to recognize where your time is spent, why you do what you do and what changes you can make in order to achieve self-actualization.

Higher forms of living allow you to transcend your need to spend the majority of your time working for someone else—meaning you are working for their dreams, not yours—and make the shift in your life to achieve a dream that you hold dear. As children, we grow up learning to crawl before we walk, and walk before we run, and yet many adults live their lives at a complete standstill, not running or even walking to higher levels of consciousness, higher levels of financial independence, higher-quality relationships. Higher levels of consciousness allow us to understand why we do what we do, to make the necessary changes and modify our choices based upon this higher level of awareness, and thus, to manifest who we are, what we do, what we have, and what we ultimately achieve in our lives.

Through the stories that are to unfold in the coming chapters, I will attempt to demonstrate that many of our experiences and the circumstances that follow these events are mostly self-inflicted, though some are out of our control. Many of you will be able to identify with the stories I'll tell because similar events have taken place in your own life. For others, these chapters will bring new information into your life and hopefully help you either reconstruct your existing reality or altogether shift your consciousness in a completely new direction, ultimately towards a life of higher living in the broadest sense possible. That is to say for example, that your incredible levels of financial success, if accompanied by utter lack of awareness of what constitutes a healthy lifestyle, will not be considered "higher living in the broadest sense." It is fair to say that becoming fully self-actualized means reaching a state of excellent balance in your life and eliminating significant segment deficiencies.

OPERATING FROM FEAR: THE POWER OF THE MIND

The picture of your future is framed & hanging in your mind. You must only unlock your mind so as to see it.

Glenn Gary

The mind as we know it is incredibly powerful, and yet many people do not use the power of their minds to manifest and change their reality. Fear is a part of the mind and also plays a strong role in many of the decisions that we make. To give you an example of just how powerful the mind is and how fear can play a role in these decisions, I will share a recent prank that one of my friends played on me with magnificent success.

My friend decided to spin a story that he carefully orchestrated with precision. On a Thursday night he called and we talked for a few minutes about his kids, work and general catching up as we had not talked for more than a week. During our conversation he asked if I had heard about the serial killer that was supposedly on the loose in our area. He went on to describe the killer as having committed four murders, execution-style. The killer would drive up on a motorcycle, dressed in black, and assassinate the people using a silencer. My friend went into great detail and he made a point to say, "Glenn, given that you drive that flashy convertible of yours, you may want to be extra careful."

I informed him that I had not heard about it in the news, and he replied that police were keeping the details pretty quiet until they could determine what connection the victims had with each other. I remember making a point that the killer probably knew the victims based on the fact that robbery was not the intent (something I knew because my friend made a point of mentioning it). As we ended our conversation we agreed to meet for lunch the next day. Of course that night I had to go onto Google to see if I could find that local story.

Like clockwork, he called the next day and said that when he arrived at the restaurant which was just down the street from my house, he would call me. Sure enough a few hours later he called to say that he was at the restaurant, so I quickly shut down the computer and scrambled for my things. As I walked out the front door, I saw a person dressed in black pull into my driveway on a motorcycle. Everything happened so quickly that it was like a blur. He got off the bike, and without time to think, my adrenaline kicked in, and for a split second I felt as if someone was trying to kill me.

I have never felt such fear before in my life, and all I could think of was to run, run as fast as I could. Fortunately I was not wearing a suit and tie that day but was dressed for the occasion; my running shoes and shorts made my flight for my life that much easier. I ran across the front of my yard, jumped off the yard onto the sidewalk and scraped my arm on the neighbors' cement pillar, and made a mad dash for the street.

The fear was intense. I crossed the street in front of oncoming traffic, heading for the parking lot. The sight of this menacing motorcyclist, with black pants, black shoes, black leather jacket, and black helmet made me feel as though the grim reaper had come calling.

It was not until I was at a safe enough distance in the parking lot that I could look back and see this masked man take off the helmet and clutch his stomach with laughter. Now that I had stopped running, my mind could finally process what was happening, and I could see that this was indeed my friend, who by now was on my front yard, doubled over in grand delight at how the prank had been executed so well. Of course he had been wearing a helmet, and I was not at all aware that my friend owned a motorcycle.

I went from fearing for my life to being thankful, and then to utter embarrassment that I had been so completely hoodwinked. As I processed these events in my mind, I realized that our minds operate out of fear, meaning that we seek to avoid that which scares us. In essence we play life very safely. For example, a small percentage of people will choose to jump out of airplanes, but most will not confront this fear. I found it fascinating while I had lunch with my friend, after cleaning up the blood from my bruised arm, how a person could internalize information and, at a moments notice, react to that information in absolute fear. I acted upon my fear of a killer on the loose, fitting that description onto someone now just a few feet from me, with an overwhelming and intense fear reaction.

Taken on a micro level, this story illuminates a far greater issue. We all have fears that we have held onto since early childhood. Our parents may have instilled in us that we need to get a safe job, be married and have kids, so achieving anything less is falling short. If we confront our fears and harness the power of our minds, we can live the life that we feel is important.

I submit to you that we can choose to be fully conscious and make decisions in our life based upon a greater awareness, or we can choose to subconsciously hold onto limiting fears. The power that we have in our minds will determine whether or not we move away from all things in life that are not working, unafraid of what the next chapter will bring. On a micro and macro level, we are often guided by false fears that other people have instilled in us. These false fears cause us to react negatively to things like friends dressed in black or an alternative lifestyle, which don't merit fear.

> *To walk the path of higher living is to walk the path of greater awareness*
>
> Glenn Gary

WHY AMERICANS ARE SO UNHAPPY

A great delta exists between those who say they want to change their lives and those who actually do. Those who do make a change have begun the process with self-acceptance. Once there, they can now make the conscious choice to change their lives, improve their health, find better relationships, identify their purpose for living and become students of themselves.

Glenn Gary

I have often asked myself this question: what is it about our country that makes so many of us unhappy? It is estimated that we spend over $9.6 billion annually in this country to find these answers, in books, seminars, and so on. Why do we spend so much to find answers? I believe this is due to the fact that life in the United States is not easy for many of us, and finding happiness is becoming much harder in this country. In fact, a recent scientific survey of international happiness ranks the U.S. a distant 23rd, well behind Canada and Costa Rica, in levels of happiness. Denmark, a nation of just five and a half million people, was again ranked the number one country, as it has been during most of the past 30 years.

Adrian White, a social psychologist at Leicester University in England, analyzed data published by UNESCO, the CIA, the New Economics Foundation and several other groups to create a global projection of well-being: the first world map of happiness.

The 20 happiest nations in the world were reported to be:

1. Denmark
2. Switzerland
3. Austria
4. Iceland
5. The Bahamas
6. Finland
7. Sweden
8. Bhutan
9. Brunei
10. Canada
11. Ireland
12. Luxembourg
13. Costa Rica
14. Malta
15. The Netherlands
16. Antigua and Barbuda
17. Malaysia
18. New Zealand
19. Norway
20. The Seychelles
Other notable results include:
23. USA
35. Germany
41. UK
62. France
82. China
90. Japan
125. India
167. Russia

The results of the study are surprising, especially regarding Denmark, where the weather is pretty dreary, and where inhabitants love to drink and smoke in excess. Neighboring countries such as Sweden are known to be healthier, and the Norwegians have greater wealth. In fact, average Danes don't seem to realize they are the happiest; when asked to name some of the happiest places on Earth, they pointed to Italy or Spain, places with nice weather and good food. But according to researchers, people in Europe are some of the most unhappy people.

A team of Danish researchers set out to explain these discrepancies, and you may be surprised at their findings. Researchers isolated the key to Danish anti-depression and found that Danes were very happy with their life due to the fact that their expectations were pretty modest. This is not to say they are lazy or unmotivated. Rather, contentment may stem from the fact that Denmark is almost totally homogenous with no large disparities of wealth, and it has had very little national turmoil for more than a half century. The country has very little violence and a small number of murders, and in general, people feel very safe. As we recall, when we have met basic safety needs, we free ourselves to reach for much higher levels, which translates into greater happiness.

In a radical departure from the American educational system, students in Denmark have no student loans hanging over their heads. All education is free right on through completion of university coursework. Students can take as long as they like to finish their degrees. Denmark also provides free health care, subsidized child care and elder care, all of which forms a social safety net spread the length and breadth of the country.

As one Danish resident of Denmark stated, "we're pretty much free to do whatever we want. We're secure from the day we're born." The fact that the Danish government provides these services speaks to the way Danish society views education, healthcare and daily stress, or the lack thereof, as opposed to the U.S. According to some academics in the United States, over 94 percent of college students nationwide are stressed and overwhelmed. Certainly in my own business life, I have coached many people still in their twenties who have $80,000 in student loan debt. It should also be noted that Danes work on average of just 37 hours per week and receive six weeks of vacation per year. In contrast, we see a lot of unhappiness on college campuses in the United States, well before people settle into careers or think of starting families. Some of the students interviewed for the report cited close family connections and finding a job that they had passion for as higher values than money. This is to say that as Americans we seem to want everything and try our best to continue to find more ways of satiating our needs for fancy cars, nicer homes, and more prestigious jobs, and yet we find that subscribing to the "more, more" disease leaves us emptier in the end. Having more does not bring happiness. The pursuit of material objects and the lack of desire to find our true purpose only tends to leave us even more unhappy.

> *Studies show that those who deploy their signature strengths in wholehearted devotion to some purposeful mission greater than themselves will attain the highest levels of happiness.*

Indeed, this is looking at the subject of happiness on a macro level. What is unique about your family background and childhood that set the stage for your happiness? It is my opinion that happiness is not the end result, but the way. You have an ability to manifest the circumstances of your life in such a way as to bring you a greater sense of joy. You have the ability to freely accept all that has happened to you without the need to self medicate or otherwise dull or numb the pain with drug addictions or food in order to avoid dealing with these events.

As one who seeks to self-actualize, identify and pursue your true purpose for living, you will see the events of your own tragic past as I do: stepping stones for the further development of the self. In contrast, the way some people process radical, life changing tragedies is as an excuse to become drug addicted. Can we compete with Denmark in terms of happiness? Not by a long shot. But ultimately, happiness is not about the country you live in and the social services they provide. Yes a free education and healthcare would be great, but you are the only one with the power to manifest happiness and joy in your life.

Most folks are about as happy as they make up their minds to be.

Abe Lincoln

TRANSCENDING YOUR EGO

Ego is our celebration of the unique talents and gifts that we so proudly present to the world. We must be careful with it, though, for once it grows too big and is unleashed, it can wreak havoc and alienate others. Our inability to transcend our egos is by far one of man's greatest reasons for his own demise.

Glenn Gary

Why our egos stand in the way of our success

Ego is a subject that many have focused on. Carrying around my own at times heavy ego has led me to search for greater understanding of the benefits and harm that our egos can create.

An example of a healthy and at times, playful ego, is that of Muhammad Ali, the former Cassius Clay, heavy weight champion of the world. He never shied away from displaying it for all to see. Though I have seen many of his verbal displays through the years, one sticks out for me. I was up late at night, 3am to be exact, watching an old episode of Jack Par's talk show, circa 1964. In it, Clay is being interviewed alongside Liberace, the famous piano show-man. There could not be two different people side by side in the world. Par asks Liberace to play the piano while Clay waxes verbally, almost rapping if you will the following:

This is the legend of Cassius Clay, the most beautiful fighter in the world today, he talks a great deal and brags indeed of a muscular punch that is incredible to see, the world was dull and heavy with a champ like Liston, the world has to be ready.

Then someone with color, someone with flash came
along and now fight fans are running with cash,
this brash young boxer, well he is something to see
and the heavy weight championship is his destiny.

This kid fights great, he's got speed and endurance
but if you sign to fight you must increase your
insurance. This kids got a left, he has a right, if he
hits you once, you're asleep for the night – and as
you lie on the floor and the ref counts ten, you'll
pray that you won't have to fight me again....

Ali always had a great time, and people enjoyed him
for his playful and colorful display of his ego. On the other
hand, an old friend of mine once showed an appalling display of his ego. He is a musician and Virgin Records record-
ing artist. We grew up and attended the same schools together. For a time, some twenty years ago, we would hang out on
a fairly regular basis at our favorite village restaurant. Long
before he ever moved to the Hollywood Hills, he was just the
struggling artist hanging out at the local music store trying
to learn how to play guitar. Through the grapevine I recently heard that he came back to our old town for a day to shoot
a video for one of his new songs. That was great until I heard
that his wife decided to get the street shut down and direct
everyone to get out of the way so that he could strut down
the middle of the village, ego in full view, a big star for a day
in his old home town. He was flaunting his ego, returning to
his old stomping ground to show everyone what a big star
he was. A much more humble and acceptable form would be
to film a video or hold a concert where your wife is not
abruptly stopping traffic and holding everyone hostage so
that you can satiate your ego. Apparently it was not enough
to have thousands come see him in concert. It can take peo-

ple like this years before they become conscious enough to realize that their ego has gotten the best of them. Especially for the successful, a humble walk through life is always more respected and admired by those around you.

Never be afraid to celebrate who you are, but do it in a way that makes people feel good about you and that does not project a feeling of superiority. You're not better than anyone; you may have more material wealth, knowledge and possessions, but as humans we are all equal.

Part 2

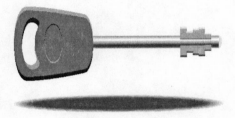

Unconscious Living

UNCONSCIOUS LIVING

Our schools do not have the critical funding needed to prepare our young to survive and thrive in the real adult world, and this is not the teachers' fault. Administrators and teachers are the underpaid kings and queens who walk among us. In order to save our children from a life of quiet desperation and create a lasting change in our broken school system, we must look to our political leaders to act as such and not as thieves and peasants of our political system.

Glenn Gary

A s I have reached what I hope is just the halfway point in my life, I am clear that for several years now I have wanted to help people as they begin the difficult task of walking down the path toward greater enlightenment. It is clear to me that if we are to walk safely through the maze of human life, we need the light of wisdom. Until I was in my mid-twenties, much of my early life seemed to revolve around the chaos, severe neglect and abandonment that I experienced in my youth. Wisdom from the great Buddha teaches us that suffering and frustration come from our difficulty in facing the basic fact of life: everything around us is impermanent and transitory. Whether you have been born into great wealth or severe poverty, whether you are mentally gifted or average, all life is subject to the following: the trauma of birth, the pathology of sickness as we enter later stages of life, and the fear of physical and mental degeneration culminating in the fear of death. Somewhere in the middle of this, hopefully for many decades, a person will live an extraordinary and full life.

The chapters and stories that follow were originally written many years ago when my first essays on my life were collected in a book entitled *Deep in the Valley*. They were dark stories that thankfully were never published. It was my first experience as a writer, one really that was for cathartic reasons. A few years went by, and my thinking on these stories evolved; I wanted them to inspire and help people, and thus my third book, *Turning Setbacks into Success*, was born. As I have often stated when I speak publicly, I have told these horrific stories enough times that for many years now, telling them is more about wanting them to be of help to others and much less about me. As I have previously mentioned, I have evolved past the point in my life where I desire to write a memoir or autobiography, for I have not done anything that would warrant an autobiography. Rather, I submit these stories in the following pages so that you may walk away with greater insights to your own journey through life. I believe that we can learn so much from others whom we allow into our lives. Looking back on these stories, I have spent quite a bit of time reflecting on the lessons that I could take away from each one and how these lessons could be shared with you, the reader. In essence, these ten stories have become my own ten commandments for living and building an extraordinary life. The life principles learned from each story will be presented to you at the end of each chapter in the hopes that you will incorporate them into your daily walk through life.

A FINAL GOODBYE

You must develop a higher concern for those around
you and for your ability to impact the world. Maybe
your thoughts and actions will drift to feeding the
hungry and to helping those less fortunate than you.

Glenn Gary

Some families can trace their ancestry back three hundred years, but they can't tell you where their children were last night! I would ask you, is your family close? Do you know your grandparents? Do you care about the legacy that you leave for your children and grandchildren, or are you too caught up in the here and now? Do you pick up the phone and reach out to your cousins, aunts and uncles, or do you only live for today? Great families are built one generation at a time. They start with one person who wants to break the negative cycle. Maybe it's a cycle of abuse, neglect, alcoholism, divorce, poverty etc. For many years I have lived as though I had no family. Technically, I have a family, but the reality is this.

From my birth through the age of 18, I lived in five different homes. From 18 to my mid-thirties, I lived in 19 different homes, rooms or apartments. That's a whopping 24 different places. In addition to making me a complete and total expert on packing and moving, it has left a mark on my soul. I often say to myself, my mother is long gone, my father and brother have never been a factor, and my grandparents, well they are gone too. I am like millions of Americans that come from dysfunctional families. However, we all have the power to change despite our families. Each one of us can say that they are going to break the cycle. Each one of us has the power to dream up and create our own wonderful families. By creating such a rich family life you will in turn be rewarded with the love of many, thus ensuring that you leave this journey surrounded by people who share in the love that you will have created. It all starts with you.

> *Children may tear up a house, but they never break up a home*
>
> *Author unknown*

At the age of eleven I met my grandmother for the first time. She managed to blow through a few million dollars during the last twenty years of her life. I can remember meeting with her in, of all places, her luxury suite at the Beverly Hills Hotel, along with her traveling companion David, who seemed to be just a friend. I found their friendship to be a bit bizarre due to the fact that he was probably 30 and she was north of sixty. She met him ballroom dancing and went on to travel the world with him in the most platonic of ways. Years later, I would travel to see my grandmother in North Carolina. Her years down in Florida had been left behind after she buried my grandfather there; North Carolina was to be her last stop. Our final conversation several years later was just as disconnected as our relationship. I was sitting in my office in Irvine, and I had called my father, who was visiting with his mom for the final time. She was dying from cancer, and everyone knew that the end was near. She only had days left when she answered the phone with little to say.

"Grandma, it's Glenn calling from California."

"Oh, hello dear," she said.

"How are you doing?" I asked.

"Just fine, the weather is pretty cold, but fine. Hang

on and let me get your dad"

And that would be my final conversation with her. My father phoned a few days later to say that she had died. So much for reaching out and touching someone. We all have a choice to write our own ending to our life's story. The question then becomes, what will yours look like?

YOU HAVE A CHOICE OF HOW YOU WILL WRITE THE ENDING TO YOUR LIFE'S STORY

THE EMPTY ROOM

Choosing to self-actualize is choosing to rewrite your contract with reality and live a life of greater awareness which ultimately leads to a higher quality of living.

Glenn Gary

I t was a warm summer night, and since I was all of thirteen years old, I was free from school and looking forward to my summer vacation. It was a difficult summer for my mother because she had recently separated from my father for the second and final time. We had left the large house with the big yard and basketball court behind, and along with it the carnage of a shattered family; we traded it for a small and depressing apartment. My brother went to live with my dad, and I went with my mom. For several months leading up to this fateful summer day, I would run away from my mother's apartment time and time again. My destination was always my father's house. I had more freedom at my dad's house, but it was no refuge from a broken family.

For some reason my mother and I found ourselves house sitting for her good friend Pat. It felt weird to be in someone else's house that night. The next day my mother said we were going to take a ride. I felt unsettled and unsure of our final destination. We drove from our small town to the next city over and into an area that was considered to be the bad part of town. Pomona is a city 30 miles east of Los Angeles and rivaled L.A. for its gang violence, prostitution and severe poverty. Over time I would find that it lived up to its reputation. We pulled up to a very strange place that I did not recognize. It had a sterile look to it, almost institutional. It was a one-story building with two other small buildings off to the side. As we pulled into the facility my mother was very subdued. Maybe she knew what was about to unfold. As she got out of the car she told me to wait. I did not think much of it as I sat patiently in the car waiting for her return.

When she came out of the building, I thought it was very strange that she was walking with four other men. As they approached the car, I knew that trouble had arrived at my door. I had a sense that things were about to turn violently wrong for me. My mom asked me to get out of the car and go with the strangers. I immediately refused. My mind was spinning. What the hell was going on here? How could my own mother allow these men to corner me like some caged animal, and what in God's name were these people about to do with me? One of the guys tried to coax me from the car by saying "your mom just wants you to come in and talk to us." As is typical, my fear quickly turned to anger.

Like a cornered cat I was ready to hightail it out of there. I leaped from the car, trying to make my getaway. I made it all of thirty feet before I was gang tackled and thrown to the ground by these four men. By this point I was scared and crazy with a rage that flowed through my body. Little did I know that I would not taste freedom again for over eight months. I struggled so violently that all four of these grown men had to carry me into the building. As I was ripped from the world and taken behind closed doors, I immediately shut down. I was now a resident of a facility that housed 30 other teenage boys and girls. They were a picnic compared to the adults that were housed at the facility. Sadly, the adults were to be avoided at all costs. You only needed to take one look at the adults to realize that insanity had taken over their minds and bodies. The staff on the adult unit looked like they were straight out of the movies, all dressed in white; their actions sent a signal to anyone who approached that these adults were to be handled with extreme caution.

They must have wanted to ease me into my new surroundings slowly as I was immediately taken into the more secure psychiatric unit that housed the adults. It would be several days before my introduction to the other kids at the adolescent unit; for now I was stuck with these truly psychotic and insane adults. Imagine for a moment what your first night would be like in this place. I had been ripped from the world that I knew. I was in a jail, but it was disguised due to the lack of bars on the windows. What lay in place of bars were two inch thick Plexiglas windows and steel-reinforced doors guarded by people who made sure you didn't think about leaving. I would describe it as something similar to being abducted and taken hostage by strangers, thrown into and locked in a strange, isolated storage room.

I tried to put together why I was there, but I could only think the obvious; it was clear that I was being "dumped" because my parents were unable to take control of their own lives, much less mine and my brother's. The irony of this situation was that my brother was living just four blocks from the facility in some little pot-infested apartment. He was nineteen at the time, on his own and trying to make his way. I used to wonder how he slept at night, knowing that his little brother was being held captive. Apparently he did not lose too much sleep, as I would find out later that he had encouraged my father to do this. On one of my parents' first visits to the facility, I made sure to give them an earful. How dare they abandon me, shuck their responsibility as parents, and conveniently ship me away to a place that housed the following cast of characters: There was John, the red headed 15-year-old child molester. I always wondered, listening to him break down in weekly group therapy classes to cry about the anguish that he felt over molesting young boys, why I had been included in that special group of six plus the counselor. Of course we would all go around the room, taking turns confessing to the group why we were in this prison and how we felt about it. It was agonizing to listen to John express how he could not control his desires to molest other young boys. When I first heard him say it I was shocked. I was only thirteen years old myself, and here this monster was confronting us with something that was foreign to me. He had such an ugly way of describing it.

I tried to feel sorry for him, but my anger about his actions took over. He was on his own in this facility, and he knew it; the other kids hated him for what he had done. At times when he would break down, the others would simply walk out of the room. It was simply too much to hear. John had a hyperactive personality that required drug treatment, and he certainly got plenty of that at the facility. Up to three times a day, meds were passed out to most of us as if they were candy. As we sat in our rooms we would wait to have our names called. Then we took the walk—the med walk. Slowly, one by one, over twenty-five kids would make the short pilgrimage to the front staff counter. They would hand over the horse pills with a small cup of water, and we were forced to swallow in front of the staff. As if that wasn't good enough, we then had to open our mouths for inspection, so that they could make sure we weren't hiding anything. I often wonder how the staff felt about all this drugging. Did they care? Was it like drugging farm animals to them? Did they enjoy drugging the child molester to curtail his evil and sinister desires? I can only look back and wonder.

Fortunately John never tried to do anything to any of the boys at the facility. The older kids would have killed him in an instant. Of course killing and dying were subjects that we discussed from time to time. Everyone claimed that a kid had hanged himself in the room I stayed in. I never knew whether that was true or not, but being only 13 years old I went to sleep each night fearful of this thought.

How did a thirteen-year-old boy, whose only crime was feeling angry for the loss of a family that never truly existed, wind up in a place like this? In all fairness to my parents, I was an angry seventh grade kid, and towards the end of the school year I had stopped going to school altogether. But what seventh grader wouldn't be angry to watch his family disintegrate in front of him? Anger aside, my lack of attendance at school really was born out of my frustration with my father. At the time that I was living with him, he had embarked on a relationship with a woman, a fellow school-teacher whom he had met through a mutual friend.

It started with a night here and a night there. I was twelve years old, yet he would just leave for the entire night. At first I would stay up late watching TV, but after several nights of this I let fear take hold of me. At my age I just did-n't have the emotional or physical strength to deal with this fear. It was fear that drove me from the house late at night. It was almost as if I was in a cage, trapped by the fear of what was outside. That fear manifested itself in me when I would call the police, on more than one occasion, to report neigh-bors that I feared were lurking outside. I was trapped inside a little shoebox that we called home, and it made me very nervous. Often I looked back on my childhood and found very few things to be happy about.

Many months later, at the facility, one of the staff members asked to profile me. He was doing a college paper on latch key children and wanted to know if I would tell him my story. I related my story to him, telling him how I grew up blocks away from the center of town, and how just the sound of the cars driving by and the street lights in my little town would somehow ease the tension of being left alone. At the time I thought it was pretty pathetic. Here I was, 12 years old, standing underneath a streetlight next to a crowded boulevard just so that I could feel "more comfortable." Night after night I would leave the house and sit under the street-light, just sitting there. It was a big blank, a lonely isolated blank. I would sit for hours, wondering what in the hell I was doing, but somehow I had realized that the cars, the lights, and the sounds kept me from feeling more alone than I already was. It also gave me a sense, even at 12 years old, that I was almost powerless to do anything about my situa-tion. It's not like I could have gotten into my car and driven down to the local watering hole for conversation with an empty soul. Nope. I was stuck, and that in itself created more and more anger. Being 12 or 13 years old felt to me like being held down while another kid kicked at me. I wasn't yet big enough to stand on my own two feet, to come out swinging and fighting, yet I was old enough to know what was going on. Someone reading this may ask, "Why didn't you just fall asleep?" I would reply: try being an adult, hav-ing someone dump you in a place that you have no way out of, no safe place to escape, and no resources. Try that on for size and you might begin to get an idea of how isolated and trapped I became.

Hollywood does this issue great harm when it makes movies like "Home Alone." We are supposed to believe that Macaulay Culkin is having the time of his life romping around in the snow, oblivious to the fact that he is truly alone. Snow would not have made much difference to my situation either way. Being left alone on many nights led me to stay up later and later. Soon my nights would turn into early mornings, and as my father came back in the mornings, I would just be getting ready to go to sleep.

Staying up all night, trying to deal with my fear and frustration, afforded me ample opportunity to rebel. Towards the end of the school year I stopped going to class and pretty much threw in the towel, much like my father had decided to throw in the towel on his parental responsibilities. We were heading for a show down. Years later this led to my father and me having the most intense screaming matches I could imagine. By this time I was sixteen and seventeen, and I knew he would never hit me. It was too late for him to try to outweigh or overpower me. It was amazing how we would stand toe-to-toe, almost belly-to-belly, and scream at one another at the top of our lungs. It was angry, violent screaming. In retrospect, that was probably some great scream therapy.

I can remember how my mouth would almost water when his car would pull in the driveway. Knowing that I was about to unload on him, I could not wait to get a shot at him. Usually I had spent the prior day just thinking about what I was going to yell at him. I don't look back on that with sadness, since it was cathartic to scream at my tormentor. To get it out was quite empowering as well. It certainly has enabled me to effectively communicate my point today in every aspect of my life. The good news is that I don't run around screaming at people.

Well before that, I had been dumped off in a facility, housed with child molesters, suicidal and drug addicted teenagers and teens that had been sexually abused. In the end it still came out the same. I was at this facility due to my parents' lack of ability to take control of and responsibility for their own lives, their failed marriage, and, in my father's case, his total lack of responsibility as a father. The adventures and drama at the facility were constant. The kids ranged in ages from thirteen to eighteen. We attended school every day at the facility and ate three meals a day in the sterile confinement of the in-house cafeteria. The food tasted like any other hospital food, horrible. Of course, John sat isolated by himself. I cannot imagine how it felt for him to have the stigma of "child molester" wrapped around his tormented head. As he sat eating his food, very much alone, even to this day, I can still see the anger that illuminated his face. He knew he was being ostracized.

There was also Steve, the long haired 17 year old rocker kid who loved his guitar and passed the days trying to learn how to master "Stairway to Heaven" and many other Led Zeppelin classics. He was my roommate for a while, as we did not enjoy the luxury of our own rooms. The adolescent unit housed four kids to a room, each sharing one bathroom. Steve seemed normal enough, just a 17-year kid who was pissed off at his mom for divorcing his dad. Sometimes we would have group "therapy" where the parents would join in. His mother came from money. She had a sophisticated air about her. She was tall, blonde, well dressed, and successful—all of the ingredients necessary to raise a pissed off teenager. Steve looked like a stoner straight out of Van Halen. If John was an entry-level child molester on his way to murderer, Steve was just the opposite: he was 6 foot four inches, aloof, and almost too cool to be with the rest of us.

There was Sherry, one of the most tragic figures that I have ever had the misfortune of meeting in my life. She was at the other extreme. Not a month would go by without some sort of suicide attempt. Her favorite method was slitting her wrists. It was not uncommon for us to hear loud screams from down the hall, as we were all housed in a coed unit with the boys on the right wing of the building and the girls on the left wing. Sherry would get carried off to the adult unit, screaming with blood dripping from her hands.

Of course, the adult unit was more secure and carried stiffer drugs that could be used to quiet her discontent. She would inevitably show up a few days later with bandages on her wrist, evidence of her cry for help and attention. She was intent on repeating this suicide attempt over and over again. Sometimes she would make it into the small classroom that was used for all thirty kids, and other times she would show up late at night, the staff having let her back into her room. Sherry never was able to function at school or anywhere else in the facility for very long. Some months later I remember being in a group session when suddenly Sherry jumped up and ran out of the room. Somehow she timed it just right, and she got past the steel door just as it was about to close and made her run for freedom.

My instincts took over and I started to run after her. I don't know why I did that when everyone else just stayed where they were. She had twenty feet on me as I ran after her, turning the corner and into the alley behind the facility. In retrospect I can see that she had been preparing this escape for weeks. She didn't normally wear tennis shoes, but today she had on a pair of running shoes. As we ran into the alley it suddenly turned into a straight run. She was now only five feet ahead of me. My adrenaline was now at full throttle, and I began to sweat as the chase went on and on. After a bit I started to lose my stamina. She was outrunning me. It was one of the most surreal moments I can remember, because she looked so calm. Her pace, with her long blond hair flowing and her feet kicking behind her, was relaxed and yet determined.

She was not going to be caught, not by me, not on this day. My lungs were starting to hurt, and I was fading fast. I yelled and yelled at her, but she just kept going. I finally collapsed in the alley in sheer exhaustion. I looked up and struggled to gain my breath as she faded into the night. It would be weeks before we saw her again. They finally found her, and of course she came back looking like she had slept in trash night after night. She was a mess. A few days later, after being confined in the adult unit, she slit her wrists again. It was so sad to watch this young, 15 year old girl with her whole life in front of her continue to mutilate herself and try whatever she could to end her pain. The memory of Sherry and her tortured soul burns bright in my mind, as if she were here with me today. I can only hope, some twenty-three years later that she somehow survived the chaos that was her life. At the same time, I would be surprised if she were alive today. Her pain was too intense, and her resolve to end it was too great.

There was the ultra preppy clean-cut rich kid named Mathew, whose way of dealing with his pain was to get high from inhaling paint. The method to his madness was to spray paint into his socks, fold them over and spray some more and then hold the sock to his nose and inhale. He would do this in his parents' garage when they were not around. I dare any of you to just walk over to your dresser and pull out a sock. Spray a bit of perfume on it—not very much. Fold it over and over, each time soaking the sock with perfume, and then hold that up to your nose—just for a second— so that you can form an idea of how insane this was. Now imagine doing that in your garage, only this time it's a paint can instead of perfume. The amount of toxic fumes that he would inhale is mind-boggling. And yet no one could ever have imagined this kid engaging in that kind of brain destruction. He looked like your all American preppy kid, from an affluent family, every advantage going for him, yet he chose to destroy himself in the most vicious of ways. I would watch him describe his technique in group, and all I could think of was how scared I would be to bring such destruction upon myself. Nonetheless, Mathew just couldn't stop dealing with his pain in this manner. He described it as an addiction. He would come home from school each day and couldn't wait to get into the garage and get high on paint. It didn't stop there, he would sniff glue as well. Mathew had a warm smile, the kind of a happy go lucky look. He seemed like your average kid from a distance. It only goes to show you how lonely, isolated, angry, and neglected some teenagers can feel, and the great lengths to which they will go to relieve themselves of these feelings.

Joey was a kid from my hometown who went to my school. One day he decided he wanted to leave our little happy corner of the world and decided to get a running start. He took off and made a beeline for the windows. Now keep in mind that these were not your average residential windows. These were made to keep you in or out depending on the direction in life you were taking. Two solid inches of Plexiglas were waiting for Joey when his face, head, and body arrived. All 140 pounds of adolescent angst hit the windows, and we all just stood dumbfounded as his body crashed through the windows on his way to freedom. He ran back home and sure enough was back at the facility in a few days. Joey was a bit hard to figure out. He didn't seem to have any mental problems, and he wasn't abused or molested as a child. Even so, he seemed to not want to walk the straight and narrow.

Several years later Joey and I were to meet again, as we shared some mutual friends. At this point, Joey had decided that home burglary was his newfound skill in life. He paid a vicious price for it. After he was arrested for more than a couple burglaries, they sent him to Chino State Prison. He lived alongside murderers like the infamous Kevin Cooper. Chino is a gladiator academy that would test him. Now he had to handle life along with gang members, rapists, and assorted murderers. Years later I would come to work for the City of Chino, and I had the misfortune of touring this hellhole. I was shell shocked at the sights and sounds of his environment. To think that some kid from our local town decided to throw his life away for an extended trip to the big house was amazing. Time and time again I have met people that just throw in the towel way too early in the ballgame. Joey by this time had now left a wife and small child behind as further evidence of the human wreckage that was his life. Sadly he was only in his early twenties. Years later he emerged from that dark hole. One can only imagine what a life he would now build. Chino had changed him and forever left him with a dark stain on his soul. It's amazing that he even made it out alive.

At the facility, we had a series of levels. One could only hope to climb from level R (restricted), which is what you are placed on when you first arrive, up the ladder to the coveted level 5. This climb took me almost a year. One whole year of my life was interrupted, as month after month I would make my way up the ladder. I hoped that by level 5, they would let me out of this crazy place. Week after week we all had to endure group therapy sessions. To a few others and me, it seemed like torture. We were the normal kids. Yes, it was true, we were a bit more pissed off at our parents than the average troubled teen, but we weren't crazy, and we sure did not have John's problem. To sit and listen to this fifteen-year-old, red headed freckled face teenager rant and rave at what drove him to molest little boys was pure hell. So many times I wanted to go over and start beating him up, to give him back just a fraction of the pain that he caused so many others in his miserable life. Of course I have to step back and, in his case, realize that he too was victimized and abused as a child. That being said, I found it so very troubling to listen to his constant breakdowns and crying. I did not feel sorry for him. I felt angry with him and sorry for the young boys that he tortured.

As months passed I finally became the facility team leader. This meant that I was given much more freedom to roam the facility. However, that was all to be taken away from me one very cold and violent day. It started out to be just another fun little field trip. A bunch of us were allowed to leave with one of the camp counselors and walk down to a local restaurant. Keep in mind that this was not the sort of neighborhood that you would want to walk around for very long. Pomona was, and still is, one of the most gang infested and violent cities in California. 12th street and Cherryville gangs brought a reign of terror for more than thirty years. The city had a huge problem with prostitution and could be counted on for plenty of murders on an annual basis. Given all of those fun facts what unfolded next should be no surprise. As our group was ready to turn back, I watched as a man and a woman who appeared to be his girlfriend started to yell at one another. The yelling quickly turned to violence, as the man started to hit this young girl. The hitting turned to a savage beating.

In broad daylight I stood just a few feet away from this savage attack. I was yelling at my counselor to please help this woman. She yelled back at me to leave and walk away. How the hell was I going to leave when a woman was being savagely beaten? On the other hand, as I panicked even further, I realized that I was only thirteen years old. What was I going to do? I pleaded with the counselor to do something. Seeing that woman being kicked and beaten with nobody there to help her made me physically sick to my stomach. By now she was laying on the ground. I was completely freaked out that this counselor would not do anything to stop it. The man just kept kicking and beating her. By now she was a bloody mess, just lying in the street getting kicked over and over again. When we arrived back at the facility, I was rewarded for my compassion by being dropped back down to level R. What I had spent weeks and weeks achieving went down the drain, all for my speaking up. I was unwilling to accept the disturbing fact that this counselor could have, with such detachment, watched another human being stomped on and beaten. I was amazed by her lack of responsiveness. To this day, when I witness an injustice, I am more than ready to react swiftly, and I am sure that comes from what I witnessed as a young boy. More disturbing was the realization that all of my friends from elementary and junior high school were in the midst of living their lives, and here I was at some locked-down adolescent prison in this cesspool of a city having to bear witness to the worst of human behavior.

I will always remember the chaplain and my personal counselor, Pastor Eric. I would often sit in his office in one-on-one sessions, and we would just talk about anything. At the time he was married and had two little kids. Often, he would share some of the most intimate details of his life with me. He was the first to introduce me to the Bible and gave me a signed copy that I keep to this day. Our weekly gatherings were helpful, and I appreciated his teaching. He did not push the Bible too hard on me and was always very good at steering through the landmines known as my parents when they visited the facility. I respected his strong faith.

It's no wonder after being exposed to teenage runaways, drug addicts, suicidal kids, child molesters, and other disturbed young teens, I came back to my junior high school feeling much older and wiser beyond my years. Little did I know that all of that horror was just a small foundation for the building blocks that would enable me to deal with the many setbacks and tragedies that I was to face in my life over the next ten years.

I came back to the facility some 23 years later. I pulled up on a cloudy and grey morning. It was 9am, and I had my cup of coffee in one hand, my digital camera in the other. I was there to take a picture of the place that had imprisoned my youth and held it in captivity for what seemed like forever. I had thought that by now it would be abandoned, but several cars were pulling up and dropping off young women. I stood outside taking pictures and noticed a young woman walk by. She was glaring over at me with the look of hatred. I wanted to confront that with a question. I asked her as she quickly walked away from me if the place was still a hospital. It was the wrong question to ask an abused woman. She gave me the look of death and kept on walking. I didn't know what to make of it until I got back in my car and started to leave.

A woman walked out from the facility with that "what are you doing here" look. She seemed almost alarmed and very protective in her body language. I pulled up and asked her what was wrong. She said that someone had reported a strange man taking pictures of the building, and that the women were concerned. I thought about it for a moment and said, "You know this place holds a special meaning to me. Many years ago I was imprisoned here when it was a facility for adolescents." She stated, "Oh, I didn't know that. We purchased the building several years ago. It had been vacant for some time, and it's now a woman's shelter." I suddenly knew why the young woman had given me the look of death. "Many of the women here have some pretty strong issues with men, and from time to time reporters come by snapping pictures. We never know if it's one of the men that were associated with these ladies." I knew she was telling me that these ladies had been abused, beaten and tortured by these men and this was their only refuge. As I drove away I thought how fitting it would be to one day come back to that place. Maybe my little collection of stories could give others a different way of thinking about life's tragedies and in some small way be of help.

From time to time I drive by the old place and smile. Twenty-six years ago life stopped being baseball, soccer, and school and became an eight-month journey into the abyss of child neglect, abuse, survival, and tragedy. I walked out of that place stronger than I had been when I came in. I walked out wiser, having witnessed the worst of human struggle. This was my own first step towards higher living. It would serve as one of the building blocks that enabled me to make the climb towards a greater awareness, a greater enlightenment. Our path towards enlightenment is only achieved by making a conscious decision to not use our past as excuses for our present failures.

My story can't even begin to paint the picture of misery and sorrow that were these broken lives, but it certainly prepared me for the struggles that I would face in the coming years. Though my life has been full of setbacks and tragedies, this was "prep school" for what was to come. I will go back and hand that lady a copy of my book, if only to say that not all men want to abuse women. I too have walked down that path, climbed out of the dark valley that was "the facility," and lived to reach my own mountain. God willing, they will too.

> **EMBRACE HUMAN STRUGGLE**
> **YOUR'S AND OTHER'S ALIKE**
> **FOR YOU WILL GROW**
> **WISE IN THE PROCESS**

A GIRL'S LAST MOMENT

I went to a party,
and remembered what you said. You told me not to drink, Mom,
so I had a sprite instead. I felt proud of myself,
The way you said I would, that I didn't drink and drive,
though some friends said I should.

I made a healthy choice, and your advice to me was right.
The party finally ended, and the kids drove out of sight.

I got into my car, sure to get home in one piece.
I never knew what was coming, Mom, something I expected least.
Now I'm lying on the pavement, and I hear the policeman say,
the kid that caused this wreck was drunk, Mom, his voice seems
far away.

My own blood's all around me, as I try hard not to cry.
I can hear the paramedic say, this girl is going to die.
I'm sure the guy had no idea, while he was flying high.
Because he chose to drink and drive, now I would have to die.
So why do people do it, Mom, knowing that it ruins lives?
And now the pain is cutting me, like a hundred stabbing knives.
Tell sister not to be afraid, Mom tell Daddy to be brave. And
when I go to heaven, put "Mommy's Girl" on my grave.
Someone should have taught him,
that it's wrong to drink and drive. Maybe if his parents had,
I'd still be alive. My breath is getting shorter,
Mom I'm getting really scared these are my final moments,
and I'm so unprepared. I wish that you could hold me Mom,
as I lie here and die. I wish that I could say, "I love you, Mom!"

Author unknown

*Life becomes joyous at that moment when we have
taken complete responsibility for all that we are, all
the choices that we have made, and thus, all that we
have.*

Glenn Gary

DON'T DRINK AND DRIVE
YOU WILL NOT SUCCEED
AT THE GAME OF LIFE
IF YOU DO

WRONG TURN

Greater awareness and understanding of others, appreciation for a full moon or the wonders of a rainy night much like the one that I am experiencing as I write this. Thoughts that move away from egocentric fulfillment of basic needs, money, power, dominance and more towards my legacy, my impact on the world, my contribution. This way of being finally has a name: self-actualization.

Glenn Gary

The police officer took me by the arm and escorted me to his car. I could barely walk, as the pain in my knee and chest was starting to get worse. My heart was starting to beat faster, and I could feel the panic setting in. As I sat in the back of the patrol car with my feet out the open door, I looked over at the carnage that I had just created. The firemen were jumping on top of the car, and everyone was screaming. One fireman yelled out to get the Jaws of Life. They were desperate to cut my friend's body away from the twisted metal. They finally took me from the police car to the ambulance as my chest pains were starting to get worse. Laying down in the back of the ambulance for the ride to the emergency room, all I could think of was the pain that my friend was in. The sirens only served to worsen my fear, which quickly turned to panic. I felt as though my heart was going to leap from my chest. I was terrified, afraid of what I had done and of what was to come.

In our lives we all make a lot of wrong turns. Unfortunately, I had made a wrong turn that proved to be deadly. I remember the first time that I met Craig. It was pouring down rain, and he was stranded, with no way home. I was his last resort on that gloomy day. I had seen him before hanging out with all of our mutual friends, but before that rainy day we had never really talked. Being stranded in a downpour, with no way home, brings people together quickly. As I boarded my motor scooter for the long trek home, I offered him a ride. From that day forward we bonded like long lost brothers. My friendship with Craig would have lasted a lifetime. He was the brother that I never had, the hip, slick, cool guy that other guys wanted to hang out with. Fate often plays a role in our lives; we ask ourselves "What if I never met that person. How different would my life be?" Unfortunately, I must acknowledge that had I never met my dear friend, maybe he would be alive today. I must accept the terrible responsibility for making that one wrong turn that cost a young man his life.

It was the 80's, a great time in American pop culture. Madonna and Michael Jackson were exploding on the pop scene. The Olympics were coming to Los Angeles. Break dancing was all the rage along with a guy from Minneapolis who called himself Prince and liked all things purple. Tom Cruise was America's top gun and Black Monday on Wall Street was coming, we just didn't know it yet. Ronald Reagan was still basking in the glow of Reaganomics.

These were good times for America. For me, hanging out with my best friend was the best time in my life. Craig's family life did not seem much better than mine. His mother was divorced but had remarried. His father was a cop, and his brother was an Army ranger. Those were some tall shoes to fill for a young man who was only 17. His relationship with his stepfather was difficult and stormy. Though we shared the same teenage angst, we were certainly very different from an economic standpoint. Craig's mom drove a big fancy Cadillac, and he lived in a huge home in the hills with horses and a pool. I, on the other hand, lived in a small house. My friends joked if you took more than a few steps you were already out of the back door. Kids tease other kids about the most shameful and painful things, without a second thought.

My father may have rented a tiny little home, but it still was a refuge for Craig, whose stepfather made him all but flee from his hilltop. Most of the time we spent our days dreaming about the motorcycles we wanted and the money that we didn't have but knew we were going to work for. If these troubles were not enough, Craig's girlfriend gave him enough heartache to last a lifetime. He was frequently brought to tears of frustration over this girl, and many a night we would talk it out. She drove him crazy with her relentless need to seek attention from others. Looking back, though, I am happy for the interaction that he had with her. Though she was troubled, she was more woman than a young man could handle. Craig's heart burned for her, and she was his true obsession in life. Every young man should be so lucky to have a girl that makes his world turn like that. Often Craig would spend his nights at my place writing of his never-ending love for her. He had a special way with words. Often he would find me the next day, anxiously awaiting my critique of his poems. The following was written by Craig:

Beautiful Things:

Mountains so high,
Flowers that bloom,
Birds that fly,
The shining moon.
A walk in the park on a warm summer day,
The dogs that bark,

Little children that play.

The pretty golden sun that shines so bright,
It shines on everyone as natures own light.

These are things that are beautiful to me–
What nature brings for everyone to see…

Many of Craig's late nights were spent at my place; he seemed to enjoy the interaction that he had with my older brother. They both shared the unfortunate habit of smoking, and I was more than happy to leave those two to their own devices, as they would often ride into the night and find their way to the local coffee shop and a good smoke together. Craig needed a sounding board, for he had way too many emotions locked up inside of him about the true love that seemed to torment him. It's an amazing thing how your first love in life can make you feel. Their romance was like a roller coaster, and yet it moved him to write the following poem.

Think of Me:

Think of me,
When others have gone,
When times get tough –
And you're all alone.
Think of me,
When skies turn grey–
When confusion sets in–
And friends turn away.
Think of me,
When the wind blows cold,
Makes you lonely–
Lets fear unfold.

Think of me,
And remember when
The days were warm
And loving then
Think of me,
As time flies by,
When things don't work out
And you want to cry.
Think of me,
When things go right,
As things look up
I trust you might......
Think of me
There's no need to prove
Just let your thoughts of me be filled with love......

It seemed as if we stayed up the entire summer. Night after night we would talk for hours. He was full of dreams like most teenagers who are too young to have lived their life and yet are old enough to see somewhere in the distant future what kind of life could be waiting for them. In life, we get our energy from others, and there is no energy greater than young love. It burns inside a young man like a fire. For Craig it was that fire that inspired him in so many ways.

You:
You're the sunlight of my day
You're the stars of my night.
You're the breeze in my spring
You're the reason when I sing
You're the warmth of my summer
You're the blossom of my flower
You're my blanket in the winter
You're the answer to my prayer

My phone bills back then must have been huge, because Craig would be on my phone with her for hours at a time. Often I would fall asleep only to awaken and find him still snarled up in that phone cord, entangled by another long conversation with her. It was amazing to see the power that she had over his attention. Their stormy on-again, off-again teenage love affair had its downside of course. When things took a turn for the worse, so did his writings:

Learning the hard way:

You gave me a vision of what life is to be
You showed me a world of what I was to see
You promised me love, said you'd always be there, to lend a hand, to show me you care.

We walked the short time that we had, never rushing a step. We cherished our time, for the time was well spent.

Then suddenly one day you weren't by my side, you were gone forever, but not a tear did I cry. I rushed through the days by myself all alone even though my anger has grown.

Then one day I thought of you never meaning to be so cruel.
I sighed for all the empty dreams that people throw away
I sighed because I had a dream, and then it slipped away.

Although I wouldn't have changed it in my heart I know its true, a lesson learned the hard way was the price of loving you...

After all these years I managed to save these precious little gems. Like a time capsule these poems are my only link to a young man and his intense desires and dreams.

Almost twenty years has passed since my young friend put a pen to his thoughts and dreams and yet these words ring out as if it were yesterday. If it's true that some love can last a lifetime, I am sure that his would.

Friday and Saturday nights were big for us, as we would often be at our favorite hangout. My friends and I needed a place that we could call our own, a place that would be our refuge from the world, from our troubled home lives. It was a place where we learned to interact with our peers, facing competition and learning, if we were lucky, to form friendships that would carry us into adulthood. Craig seemed to take center stage, and on one particular night he truly soared. It was the night of the dance contest that we had all been waiting for, and the place was packed with more than 300 kids. I was happy to sit on the sidelines and watch as he jumped into the air and landed flat on his back. This of course preceded his entire body spinning on his head. I guess that's why they call it break dancing.

He was good at it, and he knew it. There was a cool swagger to him, as if he carried his self-confidence and proudly displayed it for us all to see, yet he had faced so many heartaches and disappointments in his short life. Like many of us, his cup was empty from the lack of strong family support. I knew that though his mother loved him very much, she did not know how to intervene when her teenage boy and husband squared off against each other, as they did routinely.

Craig thought that he would live forever, that he was invincible. His sense of adventure peaked when he found himself outrunning the local police one day, as he lunged from street to street on a motorcycle that went way too fast for his own good. It's amazing to contemplate the many ways that young men flirt with death. Our last day together as friends was one of our best. We spent that hot summer afternoon lounging by Craig's pool along with some friends. At one point, we walked in the house to see his mother, who made a point to show him that she had a suit cleaned and pressed for him. It was lying over the bed, and we went in to take a look. Our standard attire at that time was a good pair of jeans; the suit seemed somewhat out of place. It would be appropriate soon enough, but I just didn't know it. After a full day of the sun and fun, we jumped in the car and headed for my place. So far we had not accomplished much that day, but we were having fun just being alive.

My last memory of my friend was bitter sweet. For a moment in time we were invincible. It was a warm summer night. I was driving my girlfriend's brand new car and we had the music on. Craig was in the back seat, my girlfriend was the passenger and I was at the wheel. For a brief moment, we had not a care in the world. We were young and full of life. On that night we were just three friends enjoying our time together. Little did we know that innocence would be so violently taken away from us. My last feeling before the hell that was to explode in front of me was just a sense of fun and freedom.

As I drove the car down a long road, we approached a corner, and my happiness suddenly turned into panic. Suddenly I was scared of how fast the car was going, and I made a split second decision that would haunt me for the rest of my life. I hit the brakes, and the car turned to the left and hit the center divider, then turned violently to the right and was now fully out of my control. My last vision was of the embankment and power pole that we were heading toward. I clutched the steering wheel as hard as I could and knew that the end was near. As we headed into the pole at more than 45 miles per hour, I closed my eyes. I don't know what lifted me from the wreckage that was our car. I don't have any memory of the car flipping over; all I knew was that I was now lying outside the car, having been thrown from the vehicle. The car was on its side, and my friend was trapped in the back.

I ran around the vehicle, the radio still playing. I hyperventilated with fear and panic. I screamed for help. I looked over and saw my girlfriend laying face down on the ground. Fortunately she was ok. People were on the scene almost immediately. I came unglued at the sight of my friend trapped in the back. The car was turned in such a way that we could not get in. The police, fire department, and para-medics arrived a short time later and immediately used the Jaws of Life to cut Craig free. To watch my friend's limp body being pulled out of the twisted wreckage was an image that is forever burned inside of my mind, an image that no one should have to view, much less have to live through.

Craig was placed in a separate ambulance, and we were rushed to the hospital, arriving at the emergency room simultaneously. The doctors were frantically working to save his life and rushed him into surgery a short time later. I was put into a hospital room, and all I could think about was what happened to my friend. Time and time again I would ask my father about Craig. All my father would say is that he was out of surgery, and he didn't know anything else. For four days this went on, until my father came into my room along with my mother. I could tell by the looks on their faces that something was not right.

Again I asked about my friend. My father stood by my bed and quietly looked at me. With great reluctance he delivered the crushing blow. He said that Craig did not do so well after surgery and had died from massive head and internal injuries. His exact words to me were that he did not make it. I felt like I had been kicked in the stomach. My mother just stared at me. I felt like my father had just told me my life was over. The life that I had known was over.

A short time after returning home from the hospital, I was on my way to see Craig's mother, father, and family friends. I did not know if they were going to hang me or hug me. It must have been intensely difficult for his mother and stepfather to welcome my father and me into their home, but that is what they did. I was still in a state of disbelief and shock and did not know how I would have the courage to face them. I was the one responsible for driving around the corner too quickly; it was my mistake that caused the death of their son. Here I was, walking into their living room, alive. By the grace of God, Craig's stepfather met us at the car before we walked in to see his mother, and in a stunning move he reached out and gave me a hug. I could not believe that he could do this. Without that, I don't know if I could have made it to the door to face his mother. By this time we were all crying. We sat in the living room, his mother and father, my father, a family friend, and Craig's uncle. I don't know how we had the strength to get through that night, but we did.

Next, I had to tell Craig's girlfriend what had happened. I had to walk into her house and tell her that her boyfriend was dead. How could I deliver that news along with the fact that I was the one responsible? But that was what I had to do. After I was released from the hospital, my father drove me straight to Karen's house. This was a place where we had all spent so much time having fun and hanging out as friends. It would now be one more gut-wrenching scene in this nightmare of a play that I was a part of. As expected, she took the news with great difficulty.

The next day was even worse. It was the day that we were to view my friend's lifeless body. It was amazing, having to walk into a chapel to see the body of my best friend. I just wanted him so desperately to get up and walk out of there. He had a smile on his face. This is something that I will never forget. He just lay in his casket with his brown suit on, and a peaceful smile on his face. That was when it hit me; just a few days earlier that suit had been cleaned, pressed and prominently displayed for him in his room. It was as if the stage had been set. In my mind there was nothing peaceful about standing next to my fallen brother, a friend that was supposed to be with me for a lifetime. There he was, just lying in front of me. Karen was there, too; my parents and I had picked her up to see Craig that evening. I can't put into words what that was like for her.

The funeral was one of the most difficult days of my life. This was not a small gathering of friends. The church had well over 300 people in attendance. Of course it made me absolutely sick to know that we were all here because of my actions. I can't put in words what it was like to sit in that church and know that I was the reason why everyone was suffering. Even more troubling was that I was asked to be one of the pallbearers. I walked over to my friend's casket and lifted it, walking outside of the church. Once I was outside and had set the casket down in preparation for lifting it into the hearse, Craig's uncle leaned over and told me that I should pay my respects to his father and brother. At that point I just froze. I was terrified of both of these men. Both were trained killers.

One was a hardened career cop and the other was an Army Special Forces Ranger. His brother stood six feet four inches and was massive. His father had the look of a man that could scare you into submission. I was so scared out of my mind and guilt ridden that I am amazed that I had the courage to make my way over to where both men were standing. I offered my hand and expressed my remorse. There are no words that work in a situation like that. I couldn't tell them how sorry I was and expect that to help in any way. What could a scared seventeen year old boy tell a father, a brother, a cop, a soldier, that one of their own was gone, and by the way I was the one responsible?

As I stood in front of both warriors I knew that both men had faced many battles in their days. This day would be a battle for all of us; they would face it with tremendous grief and anger. They both shook my hand, but they said nothing. I turned and came back to Craig's casket. His uncle seemed pleased that I had faced my fears and, like a man, acknowledged and paid my respects to both men. We loaded Craig's casket into the hearse and made our way through the streets on a journey that would be his last. The massive throngs of cars were overwhelming. We took Craig's casket and made our way down the hill toward his final resting place.

People were crowded everywhere, and I felt an enormous sense of guilt and helplessness. My mother and father were by my side for this brief moment, and we watched as Craig's casket was slowly given back to the earth. I can't describe what it was like to watch my best friend lowered into the ground, never to be seen or spoken to again. I could say to myself that I would see him one day again, or that he was in a better place, but the reality is much darker than that. He is just plain gone, and we are all left with an emptiness that will live within us all the days of our lives.

The state wanted to press charges of vehicular manslaughter, so I had to get an attorney. I spent the next eight months wondering how many years I would serve in jail. I was emotionally and physically wiped out. I found myself losing quite a bit of weight as I pondered my fate. Many friends and community leaders wrote letters on my behalf. At the end, I was told that even his mother had written saying that throwing a second life away would do no one any good. I never did find out if that were true, but if it indeed was, I am grateful for his mother's words. My life was on hold and seemed to stop that fateful day. Now a judge would decide my future. As I stood in front of the judge my legs were shaking with fear. How desperate I was for him to see and feel the pain and the love which I had for my friend, for him to understand that this day would live inside of me forever. In a split second of time, I took a corner too fast and panicked, and in doing so, I took a life. Would this judge see that any sentence that he could impose on me would be far less significant than the life sentence that I had given myself?

Fortunately he did see that. Other than a few days in jail, I was spared. I thank God that I had never been one to drink and drive, or do drugs and get behind the wheel of a car. I had been given a chance to make a difference.

Imagine for a moment that every single day that you are alive you must face some sort of guilty moment, or several moments, if you're having a really challenging day. For the past twenty-one years or, put another way, over seven thousand days since that hot summer night in 1987, when his life was cut short, guilt has and will always be my constant companion. Guilt is a heavy bag to carry around. It strikes at the oddest moments during my days. If I am having fun listening to music, especially music from the 80's that I know my friend would like, I can have one of those moments. It's a voice that reminds me that I may be having some fun, but my friend is not. He is not here to enjoy all of life's little moments that I can enjoy. I drive my car on a warm day listening to music, feeling the wind in my face, and it will creep in—that little reminder that he is gone, but I am here.

Many people dismiss guilt like a school child misbehaving. They send it away with "he is in God's hands now" or "it was his time to go." Try telling that to his mother, who put in years of hard work and love caring for that little boy.

How about the many friends and family who loved him as I did? I will be damned if I will just brush away guilt with such a quick and dismissive stroke. Guilt helps me to never forget, yet it is one of the greatest challenges that I face. How can I be happy and live a good life with this constant guilt? Many people feeling such guilt choose to self-destruct. For some it's suicide and for others it's a life of drugs, violence and self-sabotage. For me, guilt is motivation to make sure that others do not make the mistake that I made. I can serve Craig's memory best by touching others with his story.

Maybe I can touch people with the cold reality that Craig will never enjoy having his own kids or be married, become a homeowner, and other things that people take for granted. Maybe then they will think twice about drinking and driving, going too fast or being careless with their lives and the lives of others. I don't feel sorry for myself, nor do I expect or want others to feel sorry for me. I have accepted the path that my life took; to refuse to accept it and find ways to cope with it would be another tragedy. I face my fears on a daily basis. Being responsible for my friend's death, no matter how accidental it was, is a lifetime sentence of remorse and loss. Like others, for example, who must manage their weight or cholesterol levels, I must manage to the best of my ability how much guilt comes into each day. It serves as a constant reminder of where I have been and where I am going. It has been one of the necessary building blocks towards higher living. This is to say that my enlightenment became possible in the ruins of this tragedy. You may have possibly gone through similar tragedies or have lost a loved one in your youth. These events make a lasting imprint on our souls, but if you choose, I suggest to you that they can become the stepping stones to living your greatest life or they can hold you down in a sea of self-destruction. Great tragedies and setbacks in our lives either inspire us or serve to destroy us, but this is a conscious choice that we make, one that arises from the most original acts of unconscious living.

BE CAREFUL WITH YOUR LIFE
DON'T BE CARELESS
IF YOU ARE, IN AN INSTANT
IT COULD BE GONE

A MOTHER'S LAST GOODBYE

When the world is hard or shows us no mercy, a woman's touch and her smile reminds us of all the good in the universe. A woman's greatness is illuminated in the way she nurtures life; who else can make a baby's cry turn into laughter? Who else can make a grown man act like a child? A woman's legacy is the children that she brings into this world; her lasting imprint on a life goes on well after she passes. They say that a woman's best friend is diamonds; not so, for diamonds are just a token of a man's affection. Her best friend lies deep within her, the only one that can be true to her in the end. In being true to herself, she in turn ensures that her cup in this life will truly runneth over.

Glenn Gary

Nancy was a typical mom who had her kids in the 1960's. She stayed home to take care of my older brother and me while at the same time she helped to put my father through school so that he could finish his master's degree. Some twenty years later, she would come to regret that decision. But back then, that's what many women did. My parents had only been married a couple of years when she gave birth to my brother in 1962 while she was in her mid-twenties.

I came along in 1968. I can only imagine the trials and tribulations of raising two young boys as she did. We grew up in a time when landing on the moon became a reality and Watergate proved to be Nixon's undoing. My mother lived through the Kennedy assassinations and the Watts Riots, a far cry from the snow and cold of New York where my parents had come from. My father and she went to California out of necessity. They had a common goal: to move as far away from their own parents as possible. They left the frigid cold of their hometown of Buffalo, New York for a honeymoon in Niagara Falls, and then they set sail for sunny California with no intention of ever coming back. This decision would prove to be a fatal crack in our family foundation that would have a long-term impact for all of us.

As I always have done, make it a point to look through your parents' high school yearbooks. When days grow long and I hunger for a memory of my mother, I only need to look through all of the little notes that people wrote to her in her yearbook. It's hard to imagine, but our parents were once our age.

My mother's relationship with her mom and dad was difficult. She outlived her mother, but was called home before her father. My parents were children of the 1950's, and as teenagers, they became close to each other because their parents were friends, but I am not under the impression that they were high school sweethearts. In fact, I can't say that there was much romance in their eighteen years together; pure misery might describe their union better. Some people fall into a pattern of raising kids, dealing with financial stress, and just trying to survive. A woman's soul can be lost in that equation quite easily. This was true for my mother. I believe she had the misfortune of drowning in my father's hatred of his own mother and his inability and unwillingness to treat his clinical depression with anything stronger than an aspirin. Had my father been treated for his depression, he probably could have saved my mother from a life of quiet desperation. One thing is certain, my mother was terribly unhappy, and it was apparent in her face for many years.

It never ceases to amaze me how we block things from our long-term memory. Most of my young childhood was a blur. The occasional flicker of a flashback will stream into my consciousness from time to time. My earliest memories are of her putting the gate up. This was an interesting contraption that my father constructed with the use of his industrial arts degree. As a woodshop teacher, he had all the tools he needed to construct a wire fence that was installed where a door normally would be. Because she could see through the wire mesh, my mother could keep me in a contained area and not totally shut me out. Keep in mind that, in 1973, the baby monitors that we have today didn't exist. I am sure the gate was designed to keep me in time-out mode and help to keep my mother from going crazy by chasing two little boys around the house all day.

One thing is for certain, we were not the Brady Bunch or the Cleavers. From when I was a toddler, one memory that lurks in the recesses of my mind quite clearly is that of my mother laying face down on her bed, hanging over the side with her head dangling towards the ground. She suffered from tremendous headaches; they were one of many clues of what was to come. I can count on one hand the number of times that we all sat down at the dinner table together. If there is one crime that parents can commit, it is denying their family a home-cooked meal where everyone unites to discuss the day's events.

My parents separated when I was only ten years old. For a time, we had to move from our small home into an apartment. After more than a year apart, they decided to give the family thing one last try. They figured that moving into a large five-bedroom house with its own basketball court and huge yard would do the trick. I should have known that a bigger house only allowed for greater distance between my parents. Now, my dad was free to move out of the master bedroom and into the garage. Always the handyman, he thought it was pretty nifty that he had converted his custom ping-pong table into a bed. You can buy a big huge home, but if you can't bring any love and romance into it, then it will remain as empty as the people who inhabit it. It's no wonder my brother was more than willing to get stoned with his friends instead of constantly bearing witness to the destructive union that my parents had. By the time of my twelfth birthday, my parents were ready to throw in the towel. For me, there are few moments uglier than when I went through my mother's belongings and read my father's miserable and tortured letters that he had written to her. They are truly a window into their eighteen years together, and a dark one at that.

Somehow, deep in our minds, we know when someone has died. For me, I knew as I drove my car to my mother's house for the last time that she was already gone. Our last conversation together had been a good one. It was a Friday night, and I had called her to set a time the next day to pick her up. We were going to look for a new place for her to live. At 51, my mother had to suffer the indignity of renting a room from a friend. I was so very proud of my mother; here she was, having gone through a divorce, trying to raise two kids the best that she could, and now, at this stage of her life, she was a full-time college student. She was in her senior year, working on getting her teaching credential. Hundreds of little boys and girls have missed out on my mom as their teacher. Her love for little kids was amazing. She would have been such a great gift to so many students. She was also trying her best to hold down a job at her university's infant center. Often, she would take me to the infant center to see the children. I had a tough time dealing with all of those crying little babies, but my mother would light up. The sheer joy that she took in holding and taking care of little babies as young as six weeks was truly inspiring.

In my mother's life, she faced incredible disappointment and sadness, and yet, she reveled in the young lives that she held in her hands. She had found her true calling in life, and was working hard to get to that next step. She lived with me for a short time, and we made some plans for us to find a place together again. In what would be our last time speaking together, she was upbeat and feeling good. Looking back, I feel so much better that we were able to have that positive connection. When death comes calling, it is a treasure to know that you left on positive terms.

I awoke Saturday morning and called my mom first thing. It was odd that her phone had a fast busy signal as if it was off the hook. I tried calling several more times over the next few hours and still there was no answer. By late afternoon, I was worried and decided to drive over to her house. Upon my arrival, all the lights were on and windows were open. Her car was still in the driveway. Her roommate was not home. So I made my way into my mother's room, looked in and did not see her. Thinking that she might have gone to the market, I drove around the local stores and neighborhoods, but could not find my mother. I finally gave up and went home.

That Saturday night was anything but enjoyable. I went to my girlfriend's house to watch the video of a funeral for her uncle Ken. He was a naval commander, in his mid-forties, and had been stationed in Manila, along the Philippine Islands. I had last seen him that prior Thanksgiving at his home in Point Magu where he was now stationed. I could see how proud of a military man he was. It would be Ken's last Thanksgiving with his family. He had developed cancer that would take his life four months later. At dinner, you could see how thin he was, and yet he never let on to any of us that he was dying. He faced his last days with courage and with the love of his family. Now, here I was, on this Saturday night, watching the video of his burial.

The 21-gun salute cracked over the video like loud thunder. I was shell-shocked to see a life cut so short.

The whole time I was watching the video of Ken's funeral, I kept thinking of my mom. I kept calling her house late into the night, and still no answer. I awoke the next day, a hot and sunny June morning, and raced to the phone. My only thought was of my mother. I was already in a somber mood from witnessing Ken's life come to such an early end. I heard that fast, busy signal again, and knew that something was terribly wrong. I threw my clothes on and raced to my car in a panic. As I drove, I knew that my life was about to change. I could feel my adrenaline kick in. The closer I got to her house, the tenser I became. It was as if I knew that I was preparing for a battle or confrontation of some sort; I could feel the intensity pick up. By the time I arrived at her house, my mind was already made up. It's a strange feeling to sense when life is about to take a violently sharp turn. As I approached her front door, I decided to look in her bedroom window. It was open, and the lights were still on. I don't know what told me to do that, but somehow I just knew something awful had happened to her. I looked in and saw her arm; it was pale. Although I could not see her entire body, I could see that she was by the side of her bed.

I pounded on the front door and screamed for help. Her roommate answered and looked startled to see me. It was clear that she had no idea what was going on. I raced inside my mother's bedroom, my heart now pumping rapidly. I threw open her bedroom door and went to the other side of her bed. There was my mother, lying on her back, blood on her face. She had cotton in her nose from what must have been a nose bleed. A few feet away was the phone that I must have called over thirty times; it was off the hook. It too had blood on it, as if she had tried to make one last call. I am sure she knew something was wrong, and yet she was not given enough time to make that one last cry for help.

Death can invoke quite a bit of fear into the living, and so I ran out of the room, afraid to be around my mother's body. I called 9-1-1 and screamed for them to help my mother. By this time, I was yelling and feeling very out of control. I paced back and forth from my mother's room to the front of the house. Everything was moving so quickly. I had no idea how she had died. I ran back into the room, yet I still could not believe what I was seeing. I looked at her again; she was discolored and looked like she had been dead for a while. It was an ugly, almost violent looking death. Suddenly, everything about the last two days came into focus. Why had I not seen her on Saturday when I went into her bedroom? She was lying by the side of her bed where she must have collapsed, and I had only taken a quick peek inside. She was lying in her bedroom the entire time that I was driving around looking for her.

The next scene that unfolded was truly a nightmare. The police arrived within a few moments, but it was when the coroner showed up that things took a turn for the worse. Watching your mother being carried out in a black body bag is not what the script called for at the age of 20. I was horrified by how clinical the coroner was. As this man and his oversized camera walked into my mother's room, he seemed so detached from the carnage that was before him. He simply took picture after picture of her from every angle. The camera flared away. I am sure he took more shots of her dead than people took of her while she was alive. He seemed so immune. When he was all done, he calmly exited her room and walked over to me. I guess he figured that I needed to hear his thoughts on the whole process of photographing the dead. His brilliant and soothing words to me were, "boy, your mom was a real pack rat."

In retrospect, I believe that man was very lucky. He

escaped my mother's room with his camera still in one piece. Had I not been in a numb state of shock, I would have taken both him and his camera apart. Those insensitive and completely uncalled-for remarks would have been answered with a swift response. But, at that moment, I was already too weak to fight back. I had been given my own knock-out punch. His words remind me of the cruelty of people and how they live their lives. My world was blown apart; my mother lay a few feet from me and was now gone. I watched as she was wheeled by me in that black bag. They put her in the back of the coroner's white van as if they were loading groceries from a store.

My mother's life, still full of so much promise and unfulfilled potential, was carried away. She had many more chapters to write and so many more young lives to touch. I could only sit at the edge of the lawn as my mother was driven away. Words can't really describe that scene. I felt like my life was over at that moment. I felt compelled to walk into her room after her body had been removed to see where she had been lying. Blood covered the area, and it was in several places throughout her room. I would face the challenge of retrieving her things on another day. Several hours later, I called my brother and my father to deliver the news. I chose to not call them until after she was taken away. In retrospect, I realize that I wanted to be alone with my mother. In both life and death, I was the one that was there for her. I was the one who had picked her up from school. I was the one who had driven her to work. I was the one who she called to tell how excited she was about the "A" that she just earned on her big test. I was the only one. By this time, my father had remarried. My brother and my mother had a very strained relationship at best. Because of these things, I chose to be with her alone in the end; they would have to wait until I could pull myself together.

Over the phone and in vivid detail, I described for my brother that his mother was dead. He thought I was joking at first. Like most of us, he couldn't imagine something so terrible, but he finally comprehended what I was telling him.

My father didn't seem to fall apart when I told him, nor at anytime later that I can remember. Imagine getting a phone call from your son, delivering the news that the woman that you were with for more than twenty years, the mother of your children, is dead. I made it clear to both my brother and father that I was going to handle her final arrangements. I was angry that it all had to come to this. She was now in some little room, all by herself, a broken marriage and a shattered family left behind. I often wonder why it had to be so ugly in the end. The next day, I started making her final arrangements. We gathered at my father's house. In his usual over-organized, let's-file-everything approach, he assisted with the details. His primary question was how were we going to pay for this funeral?

Fortunately, my mother had a small savings account. It's pretty lousy to walk into a bank to clean out your mother's last remaining savings so that you can lay her to rest, but this was the task that we faced. I went down to pick out my mother's casket; that was another awkward and strange trip. I walked into the basement of the chapel and was struck by the large number of brown colored caskets. In this sea of brown was a very unique, light purple casket. Although I didn't know it at the time, I would see that purple casket again someday. I was told that her body was downstairs at the chapel. After settling on the purple casket, I headed back to my mother's room. I found it very difficult to rummage through her belongings to pick out the clothes in which she would be buried.

As I stood in her room, with the blood still on the

floor and on the phone, it was almost unbearable to pick something out. I knew her favorite outfit; I had seen her wear it many times, and yet it was crazy to me that she would now be in this outfit forever. As I have said on many occasions, all of these activities can certainly make someone grow up very quickly. We now had to plan for the arrival of my mother's father, her two sisters and several cousins, all of whom I had never met before. There is nothing like a death in the family to bring everyone together. That, in itself, is another strange and sad irony. It took my mother's death for me to meet cousins, aunts, uncles and a grandfather.

The day finally arrived when we were to lay my mother to rest. It was strange to have this newly found family, and yet, here we were, saying goodbye to the one that bound us all together. We all loaded into the limousine for the short ride to the church. Inside the church, my mother's casket was at the front, and I can remember how strange it was to be alone with her after the service. It was the last time that I was to be by her side. While everyone waited outside, I felt compelled to just stand there with her. The casket was open, and I knew that I would never see her again, at least not in this lifetime.

I was afraid to touch her skin, but I needed that one last connection. I said goodbye and gave her one last look. It's been almost twenty years since that day, but I will never forget how I got to the church door, stopped, and looked back. It blew my mind to see her lying there in the casket and to know that this was the end for us. My mother would no longer be around; she was leaving and I was staying. I guess it's that old saying, "we come in alone, and we leave alone."

Another chapter in my life had come to an end. I stopped at the door for one last look at the person who fills so many of my memories. It is a strange fork in the road that we come to in our lives when we know that we are closing a chapter and will wake the next day only to start a new one. Walking through the church door that day was one of the hardest things I have ever had to do.

After exiting that door, I once again found myself driving in another funeral procession. We arrived at the cemetery and carried my mother to her final resting spot. The irony of this spot was not lost on me; it was just two short years earlier and only 100 feet away that my mother and I had gathered to say goodbye to my friend Craig. It was an awesome visual; my mother had stood in the very place she would be laid to rest one day. At the time, she was so full of life, and yet here she was today. Some friends from her work were there, and everyone was crying.

There is nothing like watching your parent being lowered into the ground to snap you out of any immature or naive thoughts you have about reality and the seriousness of life. As I watched, I felt vacant, totally depleted of any energy. Her sisters and father, whom she had not seen in many, many years, were left to say goodbye and perhaps wonder why it all turned out this way. They were so distant, so far away and so removed. Which is what death brings us: reflection. Suddenly, as if the fog in our lives has been lifted, we see relationships, grudges, and broken bonds with family in a whole new light. It's as if things finally come into focus. People must ask the simple question: why should someone have to die before we all gather around them? It's a lesson that people do not learn until it's too late.

The years ahead would see me return many times to the spot where my fallen friend and mother are lying. The ritual is usually the same; I visit with Craig and have to fight back my emotions. All it takes is reading his tombstone: *"May he dwell in the house of the Lord, where pain and sorrow are no more, but life is everlasting,"* to send me running for my car. The intensity of him being gone is too much.

With my mother it's a different kind of sadness, a bitterness about how difficult her life was. It's looking back on all of her intense struggles just to survive each day. It's the many people that she could have touched and the many children that would have benefited from her loving embrace and special teachings. It's a life that was struck down and not fully lived. I can only hope that she left the world something positive, a son who will never forget her, who would keep her life and spirit alive and use what she had taught him to make the world just a little better in his own way; that's what she would have wanted.

Death brings us great adversity. We react to that adversity in one of two ways. It can weaken us to a point where we break down and choose to throw in the towel in life. Or, it can give us tremendous strength and perseverance, as it has done for me. When the mess hits the fan and friends and family start dropping around you, you can either gain great strength or allow it to eat you up. I remember a very strange conversation that my mother and I had a couple of weeks before her death. We were talking about the shooting death of Rebecca Schaefer, the actress who played alongside Pam Dawber in the series, *My Sister Sam*. I turned to my mother and said how depressing it was that people were buried in that tiny, dark little small town cemetery. I asked her where she would want to be buried. I don't know why I asked such a question, but I did. She looked right into my eyes, smiled, and said she would want to be wherever I wanted her to be. She said it with such a warm, easy-going smile.

It was almost as if that conversation was meant to be. I guess in some small way, it's comforting to know that she is where I would want her to be, in a place of beauty and peace. She lies under a beautiful tree, and I know that she no longer has any more pain. I am confident that her life is everlasting, and I am assured that she dwells in the house of the Lord.

Nineteen years have gone by since my mother's passing, and I only wish that she could have had the strength of consciousness to make radical changes in her health during her thirties and forties. I believe this could have saved her from dying so young. Millions of men and women alike are severely overweight, living with the risk of suffering from a heart attack or stroke. The old adage fits: many people will only become ready to make a change when they're "sick and tired of being sick and tired." This is when people usually decide to take massive action in their lives and incorporate healthy eating and exercising, so that they do not become another grim statistic as Nancy did.

> **TAKE CARE OF YOUR HEALTH TREAT YOUR BODY AS A TEMPLE. IF YOU DO, YOU WILL LIVE A LONG LIFE.**

COCAINE HIGHWAY

Too many parents let their kids wander through life
without clear direction, love and support. The price
they and society will pay for this neglect is huge.

Glenn Gary

I watched my brother Steve become a true prisoner of drug addiction. I will never forget watching him slice up cocaine like it was tomatoes going into a pot of spaghetti sauce. The look in his eyes as he eagerly awaited the line that he would snort up his nose was that of a dying man wandering in the desert, searching for water. It's sad to see our kid's baby pictures and then what some look like years later, strung out, doped up and addicted.

Six years separated my brother and me, but it felt like an entire generation. When I was sixteen and just learning to drive, he was twenty-two and coming up with increasingly creative ways to be a small-time dope peddler. He was always looking for more ways to "cut" his cocaine so that he could make just a bit more on the next sale. I can remember many days when he would come home eager to show his little brother the cocaine that he had just scored. Being that he had roommates he needed to keep things private. He would take me into the bathroom, and I would watch him pull out a large piece of glass and use it to cut the cocaine. It was a trip to watch him cut a small straw and proceed to snort it up his nose. Truly amazing! Steve graduated from our small, clean and prestigious college town only to leave for *The Islands*. This was a small vicious section of Pomona, California that rivals Watts. Pomona gangs like

"Cherryville" and "12ᵗʰ Street" were notorious and deadly.

But it's not hard to see why I followed my older brother around like a lost dog looking for a treat. He would swing by in his souped-up car, the rock band Journey blasting on the stereo, looking to hang out with his younger brother. Ultimately, though, his little joy rides back to the hood made a young kid grow up fast. I was only thirteen at the time, but watching the way my brother got loaded and partied with his friends was enough to make me see the light. Though the cast of characters was ever-changing, the menu each night was steady: lots of beer, pot, loud music, cigarettes and occasionally white lines, should any of them have had enough money to spring for such a luxury. Even as a teenager, I was cognizant enough to realize that my brother was only trying to drown his pain in all that dope and booze. Witnessing this was a good experience and laid out a very distinct fork in the road for me. Down one road was a clean cut existence in which drugs were not used to deal with one's problems, suits were worn to work, and one carried himself in a classy manner. The other road was a drug-filled one with twists and turns that would take its passenger down a dope-driven cocaine highway.

Witnessing my brother's self-destruction first hand showed me that I wanted no part in such a lifestyle. I could easily see the wreckage that was Steve's life. That was more than enough for me. Years later, it caught up with him. He lost half of his tongue to cancer, the obvious result of starting to smoke cigarettes at twelve, pot at thirteen and cocaine by the time he was old enough to drive. For a time, Steve thought his drug dealing was pretty nifty. I will never forget how he would bring his bags of pot into the living room when my dad wasn't home. He'd educate me on how much a dime bag was worth or how a quarter pound could go for $400. His favorite thing was to show me how he weighed his pot with his portable scale. He took that darn thing with him everywhere that he went.

One day, Steve and his friend Mike were driving home from high school on their motor scooters when a car suddenly raced alongside them. As my brother looked over he saw the car door swing open and strike Mike. My brother was fortunate to avoid the car that was obviously trying to kill both of them. Mike was not so lucky. He lost a kidney and nearly died. Years later, Mike received a settlement of more than $300,000. He used this, unfortunately, to further his drug dealing. I don't know why, but my brother was more than happy to continue playing a role in that nonsense. He was happy to be Mike's loyal drug dealing assistant. All I knew was that I wanted to get as far away from all of that as possible.

In retrospect, Steve was just a victim of his environment. I think his life could have been much better had he learned to properly examine his problems, or been blessed with a strong and supportive father figure. He and I were different in that I always chose to deal with my problems or setbacks in life head on and didn't drown my pain in alcohol or drugs. I faced my challenges with a sober mind. Many people try to drink, snort, or smoke away their problems, only to bring even more problems unto themselves. That being said, his life might also have been different if my father had been more proactive from the time Steve became an adolescent. Where was my dad at his soccer games? Did he get Steve into baseball, tennis or some other creative and positive outlet? Unfortunately, the answer is no. Dad was mired in his own mess and did not get involved with his kids. I have a very simple formula for success: get highly involved with your kids and they will have a good chance of turning out well adjusted. If you ignore them, they may fall prey to the outside world of drugs and other horrors.

To use an analogy, it's like going to a pet store, buying a dog, bringing him home and just basically providing a bowl of water and some food. During the day you're too busy with the drama and dysfunctional nonsense of your own life to be a good pet owner, so the dog wanders around all day, not getting much attention or love. You can also forget about trips to the park or good walks together. That's just what my dad was like. I wonder how he can ask why Steve turned into a drug addict.

Over twenty years have passed since the days I watched Steve get high and snort cocaine. He has had two wives and is the father of three children. He struggles on a month-to-month basis to keep his head above water and pay his bills. His years of smoking and drug abuse have made it difficult, but not impossible, for the two of us to communicate. With cancer in his rear view mirror, Steve and I have been able to enjoy spirited games of tennis and a deeper connection. Though we are quite different, coming to grips with our past and my ability to accept him and love him for who he is makes my life that much richer today. Indeed he has survived his trip on the cocaine highway. My hope is that you will find the courage to do so as well should you find yourself with the same challenge.

LEARN TO FACE YOUR PROBLEMS WITH A SOBER MIND AND A THIRST FOR PERSONAL GROWTH

A FRONT ROW SEAT

My hope is that people will slow down and think twice before getting behind the wheel of a 4,000 pound guided missile that we call a vehicle. For the love of God, women, don't drive and do your make-up at the same time; it could cost you your life. Teenagers and adults alike, don't drink and drive, because you may kill someone with a family that loves them. We all need to remember that if a car can kill Princess Diana and James Dean, to name a few, it can kill you.

Glenn Gary

I was hired by the City of Chino to be their drug prevention speaker. I was only twenty years old, but I had already been speaking for two years. Most of my public speaking at that time was done for groups like M.A.D.D. (Mothers Against Drunk Driving) and various community groups. My job with the city was to teach tenth grade high school kids about the dangers of drugs, drinking and driving. As I had just found my mother dead in her room, I was also able to weave that story into my presentation to the young minds that I would be in charge of each day. I spoke at many of the local high schools and in front of hundreds of kids, but it was one girl in particular from one high school that will always live in my mind.

Alison was in my front row. I noticed her because she seemed so intent on listening to my stories. She would be wide-eyed when I would pass Craig's picture around the room, and she listened as I described what it was like to have accidentally killed my best friend. She seemed to understand how scary it had been for me to be driving the car as we went off the road and head on into the power pole that would crush the car and snuff out my friend's life.

Craig was only a couple of years older than she was. I knew that it must have touched a nerve in her mind. She just sat in my front row, staring up at me and most importantly, listening to me talk about how easy it is to just take a corner too fast and in an instant, end your own life. When school let out for the summer, she did the things most teenagers do. Her road would be a bit different than the rest on one fateful day, however. She was driving with her boyfriend, and you guessed it, she was sitting on his lap in the front seat with no seat belt on. I'm sure she was laughing, having a great time. Most of us do when we're sixteen. We're too young to know better. At that age we are just living for the moment. We have not lived long enough to be conscious of what may lay ahead of us. We're too focused on those silly little moments that at the time seem so important.

Alison's life was like the lives of most teenagers who drive in cars: it was in someone else's hands at that moment. The car went out of control and flipped over, and she was thrown head first through the windshield. She died that day. Sadly as I look back on why my story of death did not save her from her own, I have to just wonder what it takes for people to realize how precious is this life that we have been granted. When school started up after summer, the kids in her class came up to me and talked about her death. She was no longer in my front row, staring up at me, listening to me talk. How sad that a child chose to leave us this way. Our path towards greater enlightenment can take shape at any age. We must not wait until we reach middle age before we grasp a greater wisdom for higher living. Though a case could certainly be made that a teenager's mental development makes them prone to many acts of unconscious living, It is my view that we all have the power to influence those around us, friends, family and so on, to live a life of higher consciousness in all aspects of our daily life. In the process, one will walk a truly rich and enlightened path.

ALWAYS BE A STUDENT OF LIFE
AND PEOPLE, ACCEPT AND
INCORPORATE THE WISDOM OF
OTHER GREAT THINKERS

A BRILLIANT MIND GONE MAD

Don't waste days; you don't own tomorrow.

Glenn Gary

I imagine what her last moments must have been like, Howard pointing the shotgun at her while she helplessly lay in his bed, tears rolling down her face, screaming for him to not kill her. He was about to pump six shotgun blasts into her upper torso. I can only wonder what he was saying to her. Knowing how enraged he was at her, I imagine Howard would have been screaming at her, taunting her and yelling at her for the betrayal that she had committed. It's a scary and haunting feeling to realize that I have been eyeball to eyeball with Howard at numerous dinners, that I've spent hundreds of hours talking with him, and yet this same man would eventually load a shotgun, insert it into his mouth like it was a glass of fine wine, and then pull the trigger so that his head would be completely blown off.

Dr. Howard Jackson was a fixture in the small college community of Claremont, if only for his eccentric personality and his two little pugs. Howard could be found on any given day walking his little dogs through the town or lying in the park by himself. He often dined at Walter's Restaurant, where I had been going all of my life. In the early seventies it had served as the local gathering and watering hole for my parents and their small group of friends. In some way, we all desire that small town feeling where everyone knows your name, and Walters gave us just that, and for me, even more. Every few years, I would make my way back to Claremont to spend a few hours at Walter's, if only to remind myself of my roots. It was always a time for reflection, looking back on the way the town could hold so many tragic memories for me and yet this remained a place I would go to when I needed to feel strong and connected to those painful memories.

Occasionally, I had said hello to Howard over the years, but I never once stopped to really get to know the man that the locals considered to be a brilliant college professor and a tortured soul. He had made his way to Claremont in the late seventies and graduated with a doctorate in classical Greek history and early Christianity. Howard spoke more than half a dozen languages, including Classic Greek, Kione, Egyptian and Hebrew. He had recently been promoted to Adjunct Associate Professor, a position he had sought for many years. Students and faculty alike considered him to be a great scholar.

I had just moved back to my hometown after being away for more than fifteen years when I began my short-lived friendship with Howard. I ran into him at the park where I had taken my pug. It is a strange and bittersweet feeling when you return to your hometown in your mid-thirties and to a life full of memories. As a little boy, I had been dropped off after school at this same park and spent many a summer at the local camp located there. I remember encountering Howard that day and being so happy to have found someone that I knew in this small town who also had pug companions. Finally, my little pug pal would have two new friends. Howard and I didn't waste any time getting reacquainted; we talked for more than an hour that day.

Howard and I quickly developed a routine as I would bring my pug down to the park every late afternoon. Typically, the professor was a creature of habit. He lectured to his students in the mornings and walked his dogs at the same time each afternoon. Occasionally, though, he would miss a day, and when I found out why, I discovered his dark side. His extreme depression would be so debilitating that he would neglect the pups and could not find his way out of the house. For the most part, Howard found Tiny and Mr. Biggs to be much better companions than people. It's a funny thing, a man's relationship with his dogs. They were his escape from reality. My own time with Howard was a much-needed break from my day and gave me a chance to learn about a man to whom few could get close.

Howard grew up in the early 1950s, and from what he shared with me, his childhood seemed very cold and dark. Howard's father was a successful Wall Street raider. An accountant by trade, he would buy troubled companies, slash personnel, and return the companies to profitability. The man never seemed to take an interest in his young son. Howard was exiled from the nightly dinner table until he was twelve years old. His father reasoned that until Howard was capable of holding "an adult conversation," he was not welcome to sit in his father's presence. His mother seemed to hold the same opinion as her husband. She too was distant and remote, and neither of them were interested in taking part in Howard's childhood. As a result, Howard was raised primarily by maids and house staff. It was an eccentric lifestyle for any child, especially when the wealthy family settled in the Caribbean. We can often discover a man's personality by analyzing his choice of career. Consider for a moment that his father seemed to care only about acquiring companies he could gut. He did not seem to care at all about the many people he drove into unemployment. Howard's father's indifference towards people would come to have tragic consequences for his son, but his father did not live to see the fruit of his damaging parenting. Howard went on at great length one day, telling me that he never went to his father's funeral. His mother lived back East and had amassed quite a fortune from her husband's pillaging. Howard typically did not say much about her; one day, however, he confided to me that she had died. I remember being quite stunned. When I looked into Howard's eyes, I could see the anger and rage of a childhood of abandonment.

Howard seemed concerned about what he should do with the large sum of money he inherited. He mused that even after the IRS and his two sisters finished, he would have close to $2 million. Not bad for a college professor on a $35,000 salary. I began to realize that Howard had developed quite a hatred for his colleagues. He was terribly angry with the college for his low pay and, more importantly, his lack of tenure. He took it as a personal insult that the college would not grant him the tenure given to so many of his colleagues. Looking back, I can't help but think that the college was very lucky to have escaped this man's rage.

As the months went by, Howard became interested in a beverage company that I was starting and wanted to invest a small amount to help get our initial product launched and on the shelves at one of our local small town stores. Though I was reluctant about having him invest, he assured me that it would not damage our friendship. In retrospect, I am glad that I made the decision and that we both agreed, that I would return his small investment if the product ended up not becoming the success that we hoped for. In looking back, showing Howard this level of respect probably saved my life. On one of our daily walks, he confided in me his obsession with a waitress at Walter's who had befriended him ten years earlier. When he first started talking about Jennifer, I assumed it was simply a spell that he could not shake. As time went by, he grew ever more obsessive. I never met this girl, but she was really something in his eyes. He stated ominously that she was the only one for him, and if he could not have her, no one else would either. I spent countless hours trying to rationalize with him that there were millions of single women in this world. Though he held a PhD, his mind could not accept this. At 58, he was still in great shape. These facts didn't seem to resonate with Howard, who on a daily basis complained, "I'm old, nobody wants me, I am old and tired." Our daily walks with the pugs became increasingly alarming as I realized Howard's view of the world grew darker and angrier by the week. The conversations soon turned to suicide as he confided in me his many attempts.

I finally realized that he was truly psychotic. I am not sure when it clicked. Perhaps it was when he related that he had a gun in his house and shot a dog for nearly killing his cat. Maybe it was with his ugly little secret that he often had escorts visit his house, though they never gave Howard what he was looking for. I noticed that he had a growing anger towards women. I later learned that he had been married for a short time. Though he never admitted it to me, I learned from others that she left him after a violent explosion in which Howard hit her.

After many years of deflecting the Professor's attention, Jennifer walked back into the hornets nest. She was 32 and broke, so she lived off Howard's obsession for her. Though he was cash poor, his bank equity line fed his desires for young escorts and kept Jennifer content. Howard's home was valued at almost $1 million. Jennifer used this knowledge to toy with Howard on a regular basis; he even paid for her to take three trips to Italy. After only a few weeks in Italy, she would come crying to Howard, out of money. She had nowhere to turn except to this man. She never truly wanted him, only used him in a most calculating manner. He was more than happy to tell me all about this troubled young soul: bisexual, addicted to drugs, and clearly lost. Yet his rage increased each time he gave her money, especially as she failed to give him anything in return. Howard bitterly related tales of their intimate encounters, describing them as if she considered them favors and withheld them to get more from Howard. This game proved deadly for her. After her third failed trip to Italy and an attempt to start a career as an ESL teacher, she once again begged him to send her money. In the many emails that they traded, she would revel in her casual encounters with European men, seeming to taunt Howard with these stories.

I began to dread our daily walks in the park, as I never knew from one day to the next whether Howard would be lucid or terribly depressed and suicidal, full of rage towards Jennifer. I knew that after almost ten months of talking with this brilliant yet very dark man, I was starting to get scared. On many days he couldn't get out of bed, depression having too strong a grip on him. My fear increased exponentially after one day when I tried to introduce him to a friend at Walter's. He had a dark hood pulled over his head and sat looking down. He kept chanting that we didn't care about him; we didn't understand what it was like to be him. He turned on us and frightened the heck out of the people working there. They had known him for more than twenty years and now saw the professor truly losing it. We left after only a few minutes, and I recognized clear signs of psychotic behavior. Looking into the eyes of the man every day for nearly a year and then finding out he is ready to kill is truly scary.

But Howard could change on a dime. He called the next day to apologize for his "crazy behavior," although I wondered how such a disturbed man could continue to teach his students. Howard called me soon after that day, obviously on top of the world as he explained that Jennifer was moving in with him. I thought that perhaps the professor was finally getting what he wanted. I soon learned that she was merely there to torture Howard one last time.

After Jennifer came home one Sunday from a few days in Vegas with her girlfriends, she fully detailed to Howard her weekend including a one-night stand with a complete stranger. Did this girl not realize that she toyed with a madman? Howard had reached his breaking point and felt it was time for revenge. My friends said that he was at Walter's Friday evening; apparently he asked a waitress, "What do you do with someone that has betrayed you?" That Sunday night, Howard decided the answer was to put six shotgun blasts into Jennifer. Apparently he walked around his house for eight more hours that fateful day; Jennifer lay in his bed, her upper torso riddled with shotgun blasts.

He made one last cry for help to a friend, saying that he had done something terribly wrong and asking her to come over. Luckily for her, she did not; she wasn't there when the professor put the shotgun in his mouth and blew his head off. Our small town police did not find the bodies for three days. I had wondered why Howard had not called me. It had been two weeks since our last conversation, when he had shared his good news. I learned of the professor's murder-suicide at Walter's of all places. I quickly left the restaurant, thinking for a moment that I was going to be sick. I had been to this man's house, in his presence, eye to eye every day for a year. It floored me how easily his rage could have ended my life or the lives of countless others at the colleges. I truly could not sleep for two weeks; I was up every night, haunted by the fear of how close I had come to death. What if he had called me that day? I would have gone to help him. What if I had not made plans to pay Howard back the money that he had invested in my company? I am quite confidant that had I not treated Howard with respect as it related to his investment, he would have come calling for me with revenge on his mind.

Death can come calling at anytime for us, but I am very thankful I missed that call. Never again will I befriend someone I know to be psychotic, for it could have deadly consequences. Even more bizarre and disturbing is the fact that Howard's ashes are on his own mantle, as he left his home to another friend. She and her boyfriend wasted no time moving in after the murder. To this day I do not know of a piece of real estate so full of murder and death as the professor's house. Howard's face, eyes, and image are seared into my memory forever. I don't need to see his picture to imagine those eyes and a look of sociopathic rage. I feel a tremendous sadness at the loss of life, a sadness that will live with me for the rest of my days. I am bewildered by the coexistence of incredible intellect and knowledge with such psychotic tendencies.

This story serves to underscore how important it is in life to treat people with respect. I think one of the lessons that we can walk away from in all of this madness that was Howard's final days is that the human condition is a fragile one and that it is critical to treat people with kindness, compassion and dignity. My feelings are that Jennifer was toying with and using Howard, which is surely no justification for him to take her life, but often we see in all kinds of adult relationships that people play fast and loose with the other person's feelings, and once in a while, it can have devastating consequences. My experience with Howard illuminated how important it is to treat everyone well, for when we use and abuse people so carelessly in our lives, it can have severe ramifications. I also look back to my conversation with Howard and how he stated to me that he hated taking the anti-psychotic pills that had been prescribed to him. He made a conscious decision on his part to not utilize something that would enable him to be much more stable. Higher forms of living require that we take care of ourselves, that we have self love and seek help when we are in need. Anything less is unconscious living at best.

As I look back on the totality of Howard's actions, what resonates within me is his existential despair that called into question his existence on a daily basis. I find the words of Shakespeare to be quite fitting in order to summarize Howard's demise.

To be, or not to be: that is the question:
Whether 'tis nobler in the mind to suffer
The slings and arrows of outrageous fortune,
Or to take arms against a sea of troubles,
And by opposing-end them? To die: to sleep;
No more; and by a sleep to say we end
The heart-ache and the thousand natural shocks
That flesh is heir to, 'tis a consummation
Devoutly to be wished. To die, to sleep;
To sleep: perchance to dream: ay, there's the rub;
For in that sleep of death what dreams may come
When we have shuffled off this mortal coil,
Must give us pause: there's the respect
That makes calamity of so long life;
For who would bear the whips and scorns of time?

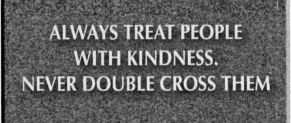

ONE LAST DRINK

*Many people in your life will disappoint you, let
you down, not respond to you in some manner. Your
walk on the enlightened path will allow you to have
the inner confidence to know that you are valuable
and important to society, regardless of whether people return your phone calls, emails, or letters.*

Glenn Gary

It's always a tense time when new neighbors move in. We
ask ourselves, "Will they be nice? Maybe I should stop
by, say hello, and introduce myself. Maybe I won't. I'll
keep my distance so that I don't get caught up in their
drama, their life."

Sometimes, our neighbors go out of their way to
include us in the firestorm of their lives. In Jim's case, the
pain that consumed his daily life played out in front of me,
whether I was willing to participate in it or not. He didn't
seem to have many friends or visitors. He was a likeable man
in his late forties, yet it was not hard to see that he was running from something in his past. You can often read a tragic
tale on a person's face. Jim's was no different. I could tell that
he had made this little condo, on our secluded county club
golf course, his hiding spot.

At first he seemed to breeze by with an upbeat attitude, always stopping to pet my little bundle of fur and say
hello as we strolled by his place on our daily doggy com-
mute. He was single and seemed not to have much family. I
knew things must have gone south for him when he rented
out the other room in his condo. By his own account, he was
a businessman who had been screwed over by a partner. I

was not privy to all of the details, but Jim never hesitated to engage me in a conversation which would quickly turn into an explanation of why his road in life had landed him in my neighborhood. Jim was still seething from a business partnership that, as I would come to find out over the next weeks and months, had clearly broken his morale.

One evening, there was a knock at my door, which always made me uneasy when I was not expecting company. When I opened the door, a smiling young lady stood before me, looking eager to greet whoever answered her knock. She wore a thick trench coat with extremely high heels, apparently unaware that it was a very warm evening. She said hello and just stared at me as if I should know who she was. I knew she was definitely in the wrong place, but I don't think she did at first. When I gave her a bewildered look, it became clear to her that I was not the one she was looking for.

She asked me if this was 12437, but of course I was 12439. As she scampered away, it suddenly hit me; Jim's loneliness had led him to make this plea for companionship, however brief and expensive it would be. The human condition demands that most of us seek out others. I believe that in Jim's case, he no longer desired to take the time to get to know someone. To him, plain companionship was like a shot of whiskey to the alcoholic, a temporary respite from reality. I could tell that Jim continued this habit when, from time to time, I would look out into the night and see a strange man in the dark keeping a watchful eye on his business assets. I never spoke to Jim about it. Why should I bring up something that would embarrass him?

We discover our neighbor's habits pretty quickly. Jim could usually be found stumbling in late at night. It was becoming clear that he favored the local hole in the wall bar up the street. Like many people with addictions, he needed to go somewhere within his comfort zone, somewhere that people would know his name. In Jim's case, the bar was nothing like the bar in "Cheers." It's funny how Hollywood can put a warm fuzzy wrapping on the life-destroying package that is alcoholism.

I pictured Jim wasting away in that little hole in the wall, desperately trying to drown the pain of his existence. He thought he could drink away all the bad memories and experiences of life. Over time, it became clear that Jim was now continuing his pity parties at home and letting them go on for several days, during which time I would not see him at all. When he would finally emerge from his dark hole, it was evident that he had been to hell and back. He would appear disheveled, and even the short walk from his door to his garage would be taxing.

One particularly disturbing day, I was on the phone talking with a client in my home office. It was the middle of a warm summer day and the view from my condo onto the seventh hole was spectacular. All you could see was a sea of green and beautiful trees. It's no wonder people like to golf so much in this country. The ocean breeze was blowing in across the smooth green valleys of grass, and it was a wonderful day.

Unfortunately for Jim, he could not see any of the beauty of the glorious day just beyond his windows. He appeared at my back porch, and his sudden arrival scared the heck out of me. Here was this man, shaking violently, with barely any clothes on. He was clutching himself as if he were standing outside in the bitter cold. His shakes were so violent that he could barely speak above a hush tone. As I was in the middle of a business call, I was stunned for a moment. That feeling quickly turned to panic. As I put the phone down, he asked me if I had any alcohol in the house. I was even more shocked. I couldn't understand why he would want alcohol during the middle of a hot day when he looked like death warmed over. He pleaded with me for something to drink. I told him that I was sorry but I did not have any alcohol in my house. Fortunately that was the stone cold truth.

I remember that Jim's visit pretty much canceled out the rest of my workday. I couldn't get over the image of this man sleeping in the dark until two in the afternoon and emerging from his wreckage only to seek more poison without ever noticing the beauty that was that day. We all have our peaks and valleys, but the vision of his dark horizon was very troubling at best. I immediately threw myself into intervention mode. I quickly was put in touch with people that would be willing to do one. For the next few days I continued vigorously working the phones, hoping to find someone who could rescue this lost soul. I did not know how, but I was determined to get him some help.

I did not see him for several days after that, and when he finally emerged from the dark cave that lately had become his tomb I was met by a cheerful smile and upbeat person. Of course, neighbors tend to be friendlier when you have your pet, assuming it's not an attack dog. Weighing in at just over 19 pounds, Bosco was no threat to anyone. Jim seemed to perk up at the mere sight of my furry son. All of a sudden the hellos turned into a love fest, and those two were bouncing around together getting reacquainted. Since we didn't have many good moments like these, I did not want to interrupt them. Jim quickly asked me if I could give him a ride up the street. He needed to fetch his car from the bar. Of course I did not need the details. It was obvious that he didn't make it home the night before under his own power. I didn't want to be rude, so I agreed to give him a lift. I made the mistake of a lifetime as I left those two to romp around. I made my way around the corner towards my garage. Not thinking, I quickly jumped into my car and started to pull out. I figured that I would load Bosco and Jim in the car after I had pulled out. I almost lost that chance.

By the grace of God, Jim was of sound enough mind and equally good enough heart that as Bosco ran towards my car, Jim yelled out "Stop! Stop!" I immediately slammed on the brakes. Almost simultaneously I heard a loud scream from Bosco, and for a very brief moment as I lunged from my car, I thought that I had run over my precious little dog. He had been pinned under the car and had frozen in fear within a quarter inch of my tire. His fear was so great that he had urinated and was screaming.

As I dropped to the ground I was overcome with the horror that my 4,000 pound car had come within a split second of crushing my beloved little friend to death. The love that pets give us is truly a blessing in life, and the love that we give back to them makes us better people. When we can love animals, it teaches us to not be selfish and self-centered, thus enabling us to become better people at the end of the day. As I lay there with Bosco I was beside myself with guilt and fear. Jim didn't understand it, nor did the neighbor who ran out of her condo to see if we were okay, but I was having flashbacks of another dark day.

I had already made a wrong turn in life and accidentally been responsible for taking a young man's life. Killing my dog would have just put me into another tailspin of grief. I was shaken with the ugly and sick feeling of what it would have been like to witness my little dog laying in a pool of blood, and with visions of my car accident and my friend's death rushing into my mind, I was completely frozen with grief. Jim was so stunned and alarmed that he too was having a tough time with what almost happened. It took several minutes for all of us to collect ourselves. Jim was apologizing profusely for not having held on to Bosco.

Though I had asked him to watch Bosco while I had gone to fetch the car, I realized that it was my fault. Of course the dog was going to run after his dad. I was useless to the world for the rest of the day. All I could think about was how I almost killed my little dog. Thoughts of Craig would not leave me. It's amazing how other painful events will trigger memories of the past and the losses that we have suffered. In an instant our lives can change. Tragedy can strike us in the most unusual places while we are doing the most routine of tasks, whether it is driving with our friends or just pulling the car from the garage. I will always be thankful that Jim spoke up so quickly that day. I can't help but wonder what would have happened if he had been out of it; just a second's hesitation could have made all the difference. Since that day, Bosco and I have enjoyed many great days together filled with lots of love, great walks and happy times. Unfortunately for Jim, his life came to a sudden and violent end. My last conversation with him was the most painful.

Many of us get so consumed by our own trials and tribulations that we barely have time to lift a hand and give a friendly wave to our neighbors. Jim had his good days where he strode by with confidence and of course many others where he walked with great defeat in his steps. All of this played out in front of me as my place was one that he would need to walk by in order to retrieve his vehicle that would somehow get him to the bar without killing someone on the way.

One day his luck ran out. I knew something was up with my tortured friend when I had heard or seen nothing from him in several days. One day when Bosco and I were taking one of our many walks, Jim pulled up looking as if he had been beaten by a mob. He was black and blue up and down his arms. I could see the pain in Jim's eyes as he started to tell me that he had gotten so drunk several days earlier that he crashed his motorcycle after leaving the bar. He was taken to the hospital and stayed for several days. I could see the fight in him was almost gone. As I stood in front of him I pleaded with him to get help. I tried to tell him that I knew how painful life could be, but that it could also be so worth fighting for. I could see in his facial expressions how tired he was. I had seen that tired, painful and desperate look in other men before; I could see that he was coming to the end of his road. By now he was holding back tears, and his eyes were welling up. I felt helpless as this fifty-year-old man began to break down in front of me. I desperately tried to motivate him to keep going. I walked away determined to get him the help and intervention that he needed. The next day I made several calls and lined up the intervention that was to take place.

Unfortunately Jim slipped away from us before we could help. I awoke the next morning and as usual got Bosco ready for his morning walk. As we made our way up the steps and out of the house I was surprised to see several of my neighbors standing together. When I made my way over and noticed the Sheriff's deputies in front of Jim's house I knew that something had gone wrong. I was told that a friend had found his body in the morning. For me Jim's death was not real until I could see him one last time. I made my way into his condo. Jim was laying face down in a pool of blood next to the couch. I stood in stunned silence, replaying our last conversation in my mind with the realization that he would not, could not or maybe just did not want to wait any longer. The pain of his life had come to a point that was just too unbearable. It was clear that he was determined to drown the pain, and yet as hard as he tried it would still come back the next day. Finally he succeeded in making sure that the next day never came. It's a stunning moment when you witness the body of a man you know being wheeled out in a body bag, a man who has walked by your kitchen window time and time again, day after day. I will forever remember watching the coroner push Jim's lifeless body past my door on his final trip for the very last time. On his final day, sadly, he was determined to drink to die.

This story illuminates how important it is for many of us to reach out and help those who choose to live so unconsciously. That being said, here is one of life's greatest paradoxes: people make conscious decisions to walk the path of unconscious living, much as Jim did every time he chose to drink himself unconscious. It is my belief that if we have done the heavy lifting so as to be seeking greater awareness for higher forms of living in our own lives, then we have a social responsibility to help others until such time that they become equipped to help themselves. Higher living mandates that we help others along the way. Not to do so is our own self-imposed lack of consciousness.

> BUILD AN EXTRAORDINARY LIFE BY DEVELOPING THE COURAGE TO FACE YOUR ADDICTIONS. IF YOU HAVE NONE, HELP PEOPLE WITH THEIRS.

SIDE BY SIDE

George Bernard Shaw described marriage as that time "when two people are under the influence of the most violent, most insane, most delusive and most transient of passions. They are required to swear that they will remain in that excited, abnormal, and exhausting condition continuously until death do them part." Then comes realty. The couple soon realizes marriage is not an ongoing celebration of celestial dimensions. It's a lifelong process of down-to-earth hard work-worth every drop of sweat it produces.

We hope that when we enter into marriage, we can live our lives together, side by side, partners in life with a common goal, united to help each other through the ups and downs, for better or worse. In Ted and Shirley's case, it truly was in sickness and in health.

I must have been all of 19 when one day Shirley made a point to pull me aside. I'll never forget how she got right up in my face, looked at me very intently and with a motherly tone explained to me that there were two types of men in this world: a ladies' man and a man's man. She made sure I knew that both were acceptable in her eyes as well as the eyes of the world. She went on to explain that a man's man was like her husband Ted, a beer drinking, cigarette chomping and hard driving kind of guy. A ladies' man was a bit more refined in his attire, a bit less rough around the edges, a clean cut suit kind of guy. She said that in her eyes I was a ladies' man. I didn't know quite how to take that at the time, other than to think that I definitely didn't drink beer and I knew I didn't smoke and yes I guess because I liked suits that I qualified. She should know, since I had grown up practically in her backyard.

As kids we could count on Shirley and Ted's place to be where we could gather for a dip in their pool on a hot summer day. Though her two kids were much older than most of us in the neighborhood, she seemed to love to host all of us. The day my family and I moved in, there she was, kindly introducing herself to me and my parents and offering us a bag of goodies, her goodwill gesture and official welcome to the neighborhood. She was facing the empty nest syndrome and was determined to fill the resulting void in her life by having a new round of young teenagers to watch over.

Shirley was a school teacher, and Ted was a truck driver turned school bus driver. She loved to talk; he was more reserved and aloof. She wanted to connect with people. He wanted to smoke his cigarettes and drink his beer, never one for intense conversation; you could always find Ted just hanging in the garage, beer and cigarette in hand, unwinding at the end of the day. Shirley preferred to have a drink. On most days she seemed to have that vice in check. But one frightening day she seemed to unravel. At the time I had been living with Ted and Shirley for the previous two months. It was late afternoon, and I was standing in the kitchen when Shirley tried to drive her car up and into her driveway. She had just left her school. As it was only 4pm I wondered how she could be so disabled from an alcohol binge.

For several minutes she kept trying to get the car into the driveway. She made several attempts at backing up and then she suddenly slammed on the brakes. I was standing there frozen, not sure whether I should run out and help or not. When she finally got the car in the driveway, she opened

the car door but didn't move, seemingly in a drunken coma-
tose state. Then she seemed to be having an argument with
herself. I couldn't figure out how she had made it home
alive, and also, how she could get so drunk when she was
supposedly teaching elementary school kids just a few minutes earlier. What a scary thought. Eventually she was having a full blown argument with herself and seemed at any
moment as if she was going to fall over and out of her car.
After 20 minutes or so she finally emerged from her car and
stumbled into the house. I met her at the door and helped
her to the couch. She was absolutely blitzed out of her mind.

She lay on the couch for a few minutes before passing out. As I watched her fall unconscious, I was amazed at
how intent she was on drowning her pain. She was very
lucky to not have killed several people that day. She probably didn't know or maybe did not care, but it was clear that
she was going to drink herself to death. Though I didn't
know the intimate details of her relationship with Ted, I
could tell that it had its fair share of abuse both verbal and
physical. I had grown up around them, but after this, I decided my stay was to be brief. It was becoming too difficult to
watch these two yell at each other and or drink away their
troubles. She was a sweet woman, but underneath a dam-
aged one as well. It was clear that Ted and Shirley had a love
hate relationship. Like many couples, they found their own
unique way of torturing each other, and yet they had an
enduring love for one another.

One night, Shirley fell asleep with quite a bit of fluid
in her lungs. The years of drinking and smoking didn't help.
The fluid built up and cut off her airway during the night.
Ted would later explain to me in great detail how he woke
up and reached over to feel her very cold body. She had died
in her sleep while her husband lay sleeping next to her. What
a horrendous way to lose one's spouse. 55 years old and you

go to sleep one night, and the next morning you awake to find that your wife has been dead for several hours.

Not until after she had died did I feel Ted's love for her. His quiet, removed and detached demeanor was now replaced with a sad, lonely and desperate man who didn't hesitate to tell me how much he missed her. On one of my frequent annual journeys back home to touch base with my past, I decided to visit him. As I pulled up there was Ted in his familiar pose: standing in that garage, beer and cigarette in hand. He was happy to see me, and yet I could clearly see that his will to live had gone. If you look at someone like Ted closely enough to feel his energy or the lack thereof, you can sense that he is turning the corner on his last leg of life. It was amazing how I could stand there with Ted that day and could feel that he was slipping. His punching bag and true love was gone. The mother of his children was gone, and therefore he had nothing left in the tank. It would take just three years before cancer set in and claimed his life.

Once again death came early, and children were left to bury their parents. Now from time to time I drive by our small town cemetery to remember a couple that seemed to live such tortured lives. Like many of us, they masked their pain in life with alcohol, smoking and an exceptional ability to torture the other and at the same time find love for each other. She had a warm and beautiful motherly side to her, but in the end the pain of her life was too great for her to bear. She chose to drink it away and when death came for her so suddenly and swiftly, Ted was not far behind.

When we seek no greater illumination of ourselves other then the simple fact that we are in pain and unhappy about the path that we have chosen in life, we choose to be unconscious. All of us have the ability to seek higher forms of health, greater relationships and new paths for our lives. But as Ted and Shirley demonstrate so clearly, many of us resign to live our lives in destructive, unfulfilling ways. The psychology behind higher living starts with a desire for greater awareness. This in turn leads to making better choices about how we deal with painful things that happen to us. I wish Shirley could have decided to deal with her stress by jumping on a treadmill, releasing endorphins and empowering her body with vital new energy. Instead, she chose to self-medicate by drinking and numbing the pain that was her reality. Ultimately this lead to her untimely death.

> *Happy marriages begin when we marry the ones we love, and they blossom when we love the ones we marry.*

The preceding ten essays have armed you with plenty of examples of how important it is to live in the moment, to soak up the circumstances of our lives in a conscious manner so that we may have clear enough minds to sort through some of life's messier moments. As I lived each of these experiences they taught me the need for self love, for being my own best friend. Watching other people self destruct brings into focus how critical it is that we not follow in the same steps. Punishing ourselves with drugs and alcohol, poor health and abusive relationships does not serve our ability to seek higher forms of living. Rather this behavior keeps you from helping yourself and so many others along the path in life. Being good to ourselves and others is truly living our greatest life. As we will explore in Part Three, once you have completed the heavy lifting of understanding your motivations, actions, and the self-sabotaging behaviors that we have all been guilty of at some point in our lives, you are now free to explore other critical aspects of higher living.

Part Three will have you shift your focus towards developing a prosperity consciousness. During my ten years of investment banking along with several years of mortgage banking, I met hundreds of people who did not have a higher awareness of these important areas. It is my view that if we do not seek a greater understanding of credit, real estate, investment, and safeguards such as for identity theft, we will suffer the consequences which will tend to spill over and affect our personal relationships and ultimately our health, both physical and emotional. All of these aspects of our lives are interconnected. Our understanding of our basic needs and the six levels of human development is connected to our understanding of finances, health, and greater purpose for living, all of which we will explore in the following chapters.

FIND A GREAT LOVE IN LIFE, ONE THAT FITS YOU, REFUSE TO EXCEPT ANYTHING BUT THE BEST RELATIONSHIPS

BECOMING A NEGATIVE BYPRODUCT OF YOUR ENVIRONMENT IS A CONSCIOUS CHOICE

This is the path of wise men and women, those who seek greater understanding of all things, people, and events. Ignorance is not bliss; it's a painful decision to not be engaged at a deeper level in your walk through life.

Glenn Gary

As I engage in life-coaching with many inner city school teachers, often I hear of the struggles that they have with kids who act out and behave badly and who are so negative to be around that teachers often say they don't want to teach their class if these agents of self-destruction are a part of their teaching day. Some years the teachers tell me they have a great class full of kids who want to learn, and other years these kids ruin the experience and seem to zap the energy and desire for teaching right out of them. As I recently said to one, "Well you know that they are just byproducts of crippled parents." The challenge in your life and in our society as a whole is that we can choose as we enter adulthood to continue down the path of being "byproducts" of crummy parents, much as my father did; he justified 30 years of psychotherapy due to his controlling mother, only to become a crummy parent himself. Or we can break this cycle, accept that yes our parents were really messed up and unable to be fully self-actualized people, and we can choose to not falter as adults due to these circumstances. It's the conscious decision to live in the now, look to the future and accept the past for what it was. We are not our parents unless we choose to be victims of who they were.

I am often amazed at how many of us use our lousy childhood as an excuse for falling short as adults. Strong words to be sure, but consider for a moment that I am a true believer in the notion that our lives are the sum total of the choices that we have made. Though many of our childhoods can bring back painful memories, I would challenge you to adopt a different way of looking at them. Think of your childhood as a battle that you won. You survived the awful experience and are still here today. Your painful memories have given you many great lessons. If your childhood was a good one, consider yourself lucky and work to understand others who are less fortunate. In my own life I have faced homelessness, a dark place where you are alone with the reality that no one is their for you and whatever choices you have made brought you to this dark room. Fortunately in that most terrifying moment, I, like many people who survive this state, found a way out and became stronger for it. My days of renting $20 a day hotel rooms just to have a place to sleep and the fear of what my next move would be are behind me, but the memories are still with me and serve as beacons that guide me through present challenges.

Part 3

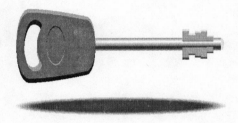

Developing a Prosperity
Consciousness

SECURING YOUR FINANCIAL FUTURE BY UNDERSTANDING MONEY & FINANCES

Some say greed is motivating. I say failure is motivating, accept it. It is how we will learn to be successful in the end.

Glenn Gary

People have such a fear of money, and many truly don't have a grasp of how to make more of it. Yet back in the 80's, this fear didn't have the same results it does today because people could secure employment without having their credit checked. The Brookings Institute reports 35 percent of U.S. employers were checking credit reports in 2004, compared to just 19 percent in 1996.

Sadly for our young adults just entering the workforce, that trend is only going to continue to grow, and not understanding how credit works, what your FICO is, how the real estate market and stock markets function can have devastating consequences in your life as it did my own. My parents never sat down with me to teach me the basics of balancing a checkbook, obtaining and paying credit cards on time and purchasing my first house so I wouldn't spend a lifetime renting. Understanding these areas will give anyone a great advantage at securing their future. I also submit that it is a critical facet of your life that will enable you to live more balanced.

OUR THINKING DETERMINES OUR REALTY

I am so damn excited to be alive right now. How about you? This coming from a man who is responsible for the taking of a human life. Let's not be foolish here. I am talking here about a life, the life of a young man whom I loved and who was like a brother to me. It has taken me twenty-one years to have this shift in consciousness. Life is spectacular, full of incredible realities, but only when deep in our soul do we choose to impregnate ourselves with this truth. This remains the chasm that exists within the confines of our existential angst. Within our human existence resides a tragic dimension, but only when we choose to subscribe to it. Your challenge, my challenge, is to emancipate ourselves from this truth and adopt a higher consciousness, a thirst for higher living. Should you not be able to vibrate at this state of higher awareness that I am espousing, I would implore you to take a walk on the beach at sunset. Rent an expensive, convertible sports car for a day. Feel the beauty of the wind, the freedom. Go to the zoo and remind yourself of the beauty that your creator bestowed upon this earth. Look at the moon tonight before you go to bed. Step outside of yourself, put down your "challenges" for a while and see all the beautiful, endless possibilities. Forget about the mortgage payment, possibly your frustrating job, irritating relationship or lack thereof and just be in the moment, alive and full of freedom.

WHY WE DESPISE THE RICH, BUT WANT THEIR MONEY

There is an insidious dichotomy that we have allowed to reside in many of us. We as a society are caught up in admiring, watching and holding great envy for the rich. Many of us say we even want to be rich. By the very same token, however, we despise them at a deep level, going so far as to assume that most of them are evil liars who must be bad people. This may not even be something that many of us are actively conscious of. If we take a closer look, though, we have subscribed to this and it has become pervasive in modern society.

Developing a prosperity consciousness in part means at a micro level that you place a high value on your time and talents, that you raise your expectations for your career or business, and that you develop a feeling of expectation. You understand that it's okay to be well compensated for your time and talents. Many people at a deeper, unconscious level feel as though they do not deserve such prosperity. In movies we always seem to make the rich person the villain. In life we seem to detest the rich, and yet we envy their lives. This is a paradox, to be sure. Too numerous to mention however are the number of movies that show the main character as the evil, greedy rich guy. Many plots are centered on the fact that poor people must somehow be more noble and honest than those greedy rich people.

You will begin to develop a prosperity consciousness when you allow and expect yourself to do well financially. Most people who are not doing well have not developed this higher expectation for their lives and thus suffer. Many are not even conscious about this limited type of thinking. All of us in life deserve to be prosperous, and yet few are. For the vast majority it all begins with our thinking and how we then proceed forward with our lives. On a macro level, you will need to take the time to learn about housing, stocks, sales, entrepreneurship and protecting your identity in addition to other financial vehicles. On a micro level, you will need to understand that your creator did not make you to be poor, sick and useless to society. Quite the contrary, your ability to manifest great wealth, prosperity and abundance will position you in a place so that you have the abundant resources to help a large number of people. The last time I checked, life was not a prison sentence for you to be locked away in a constant state of suffering. You were put on this earth to be abundantly happy and joyously rich. Sadly, myself included for many years, people self-sabotage themselves and never emancipate themselves from the ridiculous guilt of prosperity and wealth.

At night, we curl up and watch the rich and famous on TV. We tune in to see what they are wearing, who they are dating, where they live and the fancy cars they drive. We also seem to take a perverse sense of pride when we hear that they lost it all. In the morning, we get up and somehow don't seem to think that we can manifest sustained and lasting prosperity in our own lives.

As mentioned previously we have become indoctrinated through movies and television, with thousands of images over our lifetimes, starting from when we were quite young, that rich people somehow are not very honest and so on. Many of us have heard the grim statistic that 2% of our population controls 98% of the wealth in the United States. What a stunning statistic. It is vital that you examine the negative programming throughout your lifetime, whether it was from family members who seared into your consciousness this limited feeling, possibly from your friends who may suffer from their own low expectations or from your own feelings. In today's economy, if you asked many people they would blame their inability to manifest wealth on the economy. That is a complete fallacy. Regardless of how high gas prices are, how much your house has fallen in value or how many companies are going out of business, the economy is not the reason. The one mitigating factor is you and your thinking. I know this to be true for I was just as guilty of it for many years myself.

The 3 Golden Rule's for Harvesting Acres of Prosperity

An entire book could be written on this subject, but there are three golden rules for manifesting oceans of abundance and prosperity in your life, regardless of your situation, how broke you may be, or how loaded down your life may be with negative circumstances:

- Become more valuable to the market (the world at large, the company or organization that you work for, etc.)
- Help enough people get what they want
- Learn to work harder on yourself than you do your job

Becoming more valuable to the market means that you completely reinvent everything about yourself, including your vocabulary, your existing skill sets and your thinking. The market will only pay you what your worth. If you're making $30,000 a year, it's because of what your current skills have to offer the market. Same holds true if you're only making $100,000. Upgrade your skill sets, develop new ones, reinvent your thinking and resolve to evolve. The market will reward you. Trade your wages for profits. For example, your existing job may earn you wages that enable you to provide for your family, and that's a good thing. If you must, start out on a part time basis and start working on profits, developing a new business or upgrading your existing knowledge and skills so that you are more valuable to the company you work for. For example, if you're a teacher, making $60,000 a year with a bachelor's degree, consider going back to a school to get your masters. The extra $15,000 a year will add up. If you're in sales, middle management or the person who answers the phone at the company, regardless of where you're at, it's imperative that you upgrade your skills. This makes you more valuable to the market and you will be rewarded commensurate to these new skills.

Working hard on yourself means turning your car into a university on wheels. Make driving time learning time. Download the abundance of knowledge from great speakers and authors on Itunes, Amazon.com and other places. Make your gym workouts the time that you exercise your mind in addition to your body and feed it with the great knowledge that is available to you in order to craft the future that you desire. Turn off the loud music in your car or on your mp3 player and begin to work harder on your own personal development. If you will turn off the negative news, ridiculous TV programs that poison your mind and lace it with the toxicity of the world, you will begin to see the prosperity and options for your life become manifest.

Will money buy you happiness? Certainly not, but it will open up the world for you to enjoy, as you should.

Currently, there are over 10 million people around the globe classified as millionaires. That's a lot of people that realize their birthright was one that enabled them to seek prosperity, live with great peace and security and help many people along the way. You should also know that there are almost 100,000 people who are worth more than 30 million dollars. To me the equation becomes simple. The wealthier you allow yourself to become, the more people you can help and the more rewarding and enriching your own life will be. However, as we will explore in Part 5, letting go of attachments and having your sole purpose in life revolve around nothing but money becomes a shallow and vacant way to exist. So it is clear that, as with many things in life, it's about balance and how we see our relationship to money. If you want to acquire, hoard and be defined by the money that you have, then that becomes your problem. I am espousing that there is no cogent reason why you cannot have all the money in the world that you desire. You don't have to be defined by it and you can utilize it to bring much needed help to a great many others.

> *When you promulgate a lack of prosperity consciousness, what you are really saying is that you believe you're not worthy or capable of abundance. Nothing could be further from the truth.*
>
> Glenn Gary

IS REAL ESTATE A GOLD RUSH?

*Your walk on the enlightened path of greater aware-
ness is eclipsed only by your imagination, for it is in
our imagination that we build the life we desire to
live; it becomes our greatest life.*

Glenn Gary

It never ceases to amaze me when I am up late at night channel surfing from CNN to Sportscenter and come across the many get rich quick real estate hucksters promising you instant millions if you will simply just break out your credit card and slap down $400 for one of their real estate investing courses. Here is what we know: real estate will always go through cycles. The market can heat up and over six to eight years show steady signs of appreciation. But as with anything that goes up, it will come down, and every ten to fifteen year period we see downturns in the housing cycle where people lose lots of equity, and that's when foreclosures spike and lots of people lose their homes. I am going to introduce a concept to you that will enable you to avoid carrying the standard thirty year mortgage that, in my view, has trapped millions of Americans into paying three times what the house is actually worth in interest payments. Housing is and will be one of your most vital and critical assets in your life, and you cannot live a fully conscious life unless you understand the dynamics of the housing market and learn to use them to your advantage.

In this case we want to lay out a plan to grow your wealth and to help you live without housing debt. A tall order to be sure, but as with anything in our lives, very possible should we truly desire to be debt free. This chapter will also briefly introduce you to the concepts of investing in real estate at the appropriate time for your own individual situation. As with any investing, it is recommended that you purchase several detailed books available on this subject, as I did, and do your homework.

Life is expensive! 23% of all renters spend over half of their income on rent and utilities alone!!

Fully 98% of our population will never escape the incredible burdens of housing payments or rent payments in their life. Having just experienced the overheated housing run up in California from 2001 through 2005 during which I purchased, rehabbed and resold several homes myself as an investor, I have some first hand knowledge and experience in making money on property investments. I also came close to losing everything when three homes that I owned simultaneously could not be sold. My years as a mortgage banker gave me a front row seat into the finances of over 100 clients. The pain and anguish that many of my clients went through when they could not purchase a home or had problems with their credit due to financial ignorance has motivated me to focus on this area. I have also recently coached clients that have gone through bankruptcy and foreclosure filings. Having witnessed both sides it goes without saying that if you understand real estate and are ready with some cash and good credit, you will be poised to make considerable profits the next time the market heats up.

As we move through the many stages of our lives, owning a home will be a defining moment. As I look back on my own journey, during which I was homeless, a renter of many apartments, and finally, a homeowner, I find that this journey was quite emotional. There are many people who I have worked with who also at one time in their lives owned a big beautiful home and then, after suffering through a divorce, have found themselves renting. Watching my own mother live and die in her early fifties while renting just a small room in someone else's home has also made a lasting impression on me and has motivated me to write this chapter for you.

Today more than ever you cannot turn on the network news or CNN without seeing a story of the housing crash that we are currently experiencing. As is the theme of this book, raising your awareness of all aspects of your life will allow you to look at the roof over your head in a different light. It is clear that ten and twenty years from now we will read similar headlines about real estate crashes or a run up in the housing markets. It is vital that all of us step back and realize that the real estate market will always fluctuate and experience radical corrections for the foreseeable future. On a macro level, our ignorance of these issues can lead to negative effects on more than just the wallet.

If you own a home at thirty, but find yourself renting at 45 or 50, much like my mother did, it will have a serious effect on the emotional and physical aspects of your life. It will spill over into your sense of accomplishments with your life or the lack thereof and takes a toll on your self-esteem. Homeowners are typically emotionally tied to their homes; renters wonder when that cycle will break and they can become homeowners. But there is a problem with the way we have become indoctrinated in this country about housing. Though housing is a basic need, owning a home strikes a deep emotional chord within us. Whether you are conscious of it or not, the home you live in and own is a large part of the emotional footprint that you will make during your life.

Much of what we will explore in Part Five of this book will be how to lessen our reliance on physical assets such as homes and fancy cars as a measure of our success, but there is no denying that homes are much like giant security blankets. They are also like personal announcements to the world that we have made it, that we showed up and achieved something meaningful. However, with the incredibly low qualifying standards for purchasing a home that the sub-prime lenders made available over the past five years, many people took housing for granted. I want to shift your consciousness about the acquisition of a piece of land and the development of a home; I want you to transcend the typical massive amounts of debt that ninety eight percent of us find ourselves in through homeownership, as well as the idea that you now have put yourself into a state of financial security. The vast majority of our time, energy and money is spent in this one area of life.

Think about how many people you know that have become slaves to their housing payment. Maybe they work in the city but live in the suburbs and spend countless hours driving to jobs that may not be making them very happy, all in order to pay for their home. Certainly this is a never ending cycle that many would like to be free of. We as a nation have become so accustomed to carrying debt, whether it's for a car payment or a home, that we almost don't know any other way to live our lives. If we step back and think about this for a moment, almost everyone that you and I know is in this situation. Our parents were as well. Higher consciousness warrants that we seek to live a more enlightened existence, one that breaks free of traditional thinking and finds new, innovative ways to develop a prosperity consciousness. We can choose not to live as others have done.

The conventional practice of paying for your mortgage over thirty years is a good place to start. My alternative idea, outlined below, is a radical concept that I am introducing into your lexicon, one that will bring you incredible freedom and financial security. As we look at the current economic crisis that we're in, we can see that over the past eight years, many people, myself included, have treated our homes like piggy banks. We need to shift this consciousness if we are to chart a course that leads to financial enlightenment. Much of our country's economic growth is attached to housing. When prices go up, so too does spending, because of people's new found equity. Most people will tell you that emotionally they feel a greater sense of prosperity when home prices are up. When home prices fall, so too does spending on many other goods and services, and we see our economy radically constrict. This affects millions of people and explains in part massive job losses.

Rather than making this a chapter focusing entirely on investing, though, I would like to start with a focus on how to acquire a piece of land and build your own home without the use of a conventional thirty year mortgage. Let me tell you why this is such a compelling area to explore: some buyers set up their home purchases so that they are not susceptible to the fluctuations of housing cycles. If we can move you into this small percentage of Americans and others throughout the world who have escaped the traps of conventional mortgage financing, you will experience a freedom so empowering as to alter and shift your consciousness forever.

Let me show you what I mean. In expensive real estate markets like Florida, California, New York and others, a typical home may cost $600,000. This home would be a 3 bedroom, 2 bath, 1,500 square foot suburban home on something like an 8,000 square foot lot. If you had a 30 year fixed rate mortgage for 7% you would pay $3,991 a month; over a thirty year period you would pay a total of $1.4 million for the home with the interest included. Four grand a month is a sizeable burden and paying $800,000 in interest costs is really alarming. Fully $2,220 a month is going towards prof-it to the bank each and every month for thirty years of your life time.

There is a better way to secure your financial future and relieve the incredible burden of paying for your home each and every month. Let me walk you through it.

STEP 1:

We will use Southern California as an example. To purchase that same 8,000 square foot piece of land would cost $150,000. This would be a buildable piece of land, one with sewers, paved roads, existing homes nearby, and utili-ties in the area. You could certainly purchase an unimproved lot for $50,000, but you would have to spend $200,000 in improvements, which would make the transaction unrealis-tic. To purchase buildable land lots you will need some exist-ing capital. Most likely a lender would finance this for you if you could put down 30%, which in this case would be $45,000 in cash. Now that sounds like a lot of money, but think about the $800,000 in pure interest costs to the bank that you will be saving and I believe that you will be moti-vated to come up with the money using your savings and possibly some credit card debt. Now, it should be noted that building a house is not for everyone, there is heavy lifting required here, but that is also true of getting on a tread mill everyday so that you don't fall victim to a heart attack in your mid-fifties. Life is chalk-full of plenty of heavy lifting moments.

STEP 2:

If you hire a general contractor to build you a home, you will be paying more than $200 a square foot. If you do much of the work yourself and hire some experts to pour your foundation, and if you bring in your own plumber and electrician, and if you are involved and price conscious, you could probably build for $70.00 per square foot. Here's the difference on an average sized 2,000 square foot home.

Hiring a general contractor:
2,000 x $200 per sq.ft = $400,000

Getting more involved yourself,
without hiring a general contractor:
2,000 x $70 per sq.ft = $140,000

Now it also should be mentioned that this project is a two to four year plan. You will pay for this as you go along, and you will not take out a traditional mortgage or any construction loans to complete your home. The only loan that you might take out would be to acquire the initial piece of land. This project could take you four years which would require you to save $35,000 a year. During this time you would be paying approximately $1,200 a month if you financed $105,000 of the remaining balance for the land over a twenty year period at 8%. Suppose you rented an apartment for those four years, say for $1,400 a month; combined, you would be spending $2,600 a month, which is far less than the almost four thousand dollars a month if you just signed up for the standard 30 year mortgage.

STEP 3:
Let's add up your costs:

Land	$150,000
2,000 sq.ft home	$140,000
TOTAL:	$290,000

Money saved versus you buying that same house and paying for it over thirty years:
$1.1 million!

Another way of looking at this is that you will save $36,000 dollars a year for thirty years ($1.1 million divided by thirty). Imagine someone promising to pay you almost forty grand a year if you would coordinate the building of your own home, oversee and supervise the process yourself, and pay for it as you go along, even if it takes a few years. When I did room additions for profit, in which I purchased a home and added 500 or 800 square feet, typically an extra bathroom or bedroom, I always had the experts come in for plumbing, electrical and the pouring of the foundation. So this plan does not require you to learn how to do these critical disciplines, but if you're motivated enough and would like to make a spare million dollars, you'll learn the other steps: you'll hire your own labor, you'll buy some good books on construction and remodeling and you save yourself a fortune in the process. In essence, you will raise your consciousness about another part of life.

I would submit that your resulting sense of satisfaction and accomplishment will be the icing on the cake in addition to the tremendous financial benefits in your life. Let's assume it took you five years to pull this together. You will enjoy twenty five years of not having a mortgage payment and you have a property that cost you $290,000 – one that, if you're in a high priced market like California, Florida, New York, will probably be worth a million dollars at some point during the time that you own the home. You can pay the bank $1.4 million over thirty years, or you can save $1.1 million and pay yourself. Like anything you do in life, it is your choice.

Why do so many people ignore the tremendous financial benefits that come from owning real estate in this manner? For many people it's fear and lack of knowledge, but often it's the fact that we get consumed by our daily lives: our jobs, our kids, our health. Maybe you have been laid off from a job, or you are in a bad relationship that consumes every ounce of your energy and attention. Maybe you just had a new baby in your family. Maybe you're under the age of 30, single, and not really paying attention to your long-term future. Here is some basic knowledge that you're going to need if you are to pursue owning a home and purchasing a piece of land.

■ Lenders want to see at least three open trade lines on a consumer's credit report. That can be a department store card, gas card, car loan, or even a small secured credit card that only has a $300 credit limit.
■ One of the three trade lines needs to be open for at least 24 months
■ If you have tax liens on your credit file you cannot purchase property
■ You can have foreclosures or bankruptcies on your credit file and still purchase property, usually within three years from the date of the foreclosure.

WHAT YOU NEED TO KNOW ABOUT YOUR CREDIT SCORE AND CREDIT CARD DEBTS:

Let's clear up one major myth right away: having a mortgage lender run your credit makes your score go down. Not true. Only if you have several inquiries and your credit runs several times will it affect your score.

Credit Card Debt:

Your FICO score, the most widely used scoring system in the mortgage field, was developed by Fair, Isaac & Co. Most people are unaware of how they can raise their credit score. We all know that if we don't pay our bills on time, the score will go down. Here's how it works with credit cards. A recent article in the Sunday Real Estate section of the *Los Angeles Times* explained this as well as anyone could: "If a consumer has a card with a $1,000 limit and is carrying a $950 balance, he or she has a 95% utilization rate. FICO's scoring system subtracts points for such high ratios. On the other hand, if they're revolving a $250 balance on the same card, they are rewarded with points because of the apparent moderate, responsible use of available credit."

To give you an idea of how financially devastating credit card debt can be, consider the following example. Suppose you have a $5,000 debt on a credit card and because of your rent or mortgage, car, insurance, food, gas, bills etc, you are just making the minimum payment of $100 a month. Let's also assume that your interest rate on that card is 16%, which is a pretty fair average. It would take you a whopping 367 payments, over 30 years, to pay off that card! This is financial suicide, and most people carry way more than $5,000 in credit card debts. During my years as a mortgage banker I ran across many clients that had well over $20,000 in either student loans and/or credit card debt.

30% of your score is comprised of how much of your credit card balances you are using. Do you want your score to go up so that you can get better interest rates on new home loans and 100% financing? Paying down your credit cards can make a big impact, sometimes as much as 20 to 50 points on your credit score.

22% of adults are deemed not credit worthy according to a study by the credit card industry

Fixing Your Credit:

One of the most simple and effective ways to fix your credit—and one that is ignored by many people – is to simply go out and acquire a secured credit card. Throughout my twenties I suffered greatly due to credit problems that I faced. My ability to reestablish my credit utilizing secured credit cards was invaluable. This is where you pay a $200 dollar fee to the bank for a Visa or MasterCard with a $200 limit. The fees can be as high as $80 to start, but you will now have a card that you can immediately start to use for small purchases that will immediately be reported as positive credit to the credit bureaus. Getting two or three is ideal; they will enable you to raise your FICO score and begin the road to recovery with your credit. Make sure that you choose a bank that reports the card usage to the credit reporting agencies; otherwise you have wasted your time and money.

Housing appreciation:

Here's what you need to know: from 2000 through 2005, homes doubled in value with annual increases of 23%. We also know that the early 1990's saw real estate values stagnate due to the slow economy, high interest rates, and recession, particularly here in Southern California when 29 defense bases closed, costing the state $10 billion in lost revenue and about 100,000 jobs! What people have to realize is that real estate is not a way to get rich overnight or, for that matter, in a year. Considering the massive slowdowns and corrections typical of the real estate market, people need to have a 10 and 15 year real estate plan.

Real Estate is a solid investment. It has been proven that over a 10 to 15 year period, through hot real estate markets and downturns, your home, condo or apartment will most likely appreciate significantly in value. Don't just take my word for it; do your homework, purchase real estate books, and read articles, and you will discover the benefits of owning a home and the financial independence from owning three or four. But remember that housing will always have cycles that move up and move down dramatically, so it's critical that you become a student of how these cycles work. No other physical object will affect your life and dominate your consciousness more.

STATISTICS ON CREDIT ISSUES

- In 2004, 65% of teens failed a financial literacy test, according to the Jump$tart Coalition
- Teens in the U.S. spent $175 billion in 2004
- 32% of students had 4 or more credit cards in 2004
- Approximately 96% of Americans will retire financially dependent on the government, family or charity, according to a 2003 study
- 2.39 million U.S. households filed for bankruptcy in 2005
- 30 million Americans (40% of homeowners) refinanced their mortgages during the 3 years prior to Q3 2005, with over half applying the proceeds intended to eliminate credit card debt
- According to a 2004 study, the number one cause of divorce is financial stress

ASSEMBLING YOUR TEAM OF EXPERTS

When I was investing in real estate, it was critical that I called in a team of experts. If at some point you decide to invest in real estate, you will first need to develop a small team that consists of the following:

Electrician
Plumber

Heating & Air Technician

General Day to Day Handyman/ Day Laborer

These four experts are critical for your project's success. It is important that you interview several to find one that will charge you a fair price and that, more importantly, will have motivation. Fixer uppers are for people who can find much cheaper ways of remodeling, not for homeowners who want to pay a general contractor retail prices for something that could be done at wholesale. For example, there are plenty of companies that will charge you $12,000 to add central air and heating to your home, but you need to find it for $4,800 as an investor. Adding square footage can be very profitable, but you need to do that 500 square foot addition for $20 per square foot. This is a rock bottom price to be sure, but possible. Typically I would do kitchen renovations for under $10,000, and that's adding granite counters, new appliances, new floor tile and new cabinets. The pros will charge you $30,000 or more. A few tips will help you get started. We will use a 500 square foot addition as our pricing example, one that I was able to do for around $10,000:

- Home Depot has excellent kitchen cabinets for $1,600 to $2,500.
- Find a day laborer that you can pay a decent wage of $10 to $15.00 per hour
- You can pay as little as $6 per square foot for your foundation or slab
- Material for framing can cost as little as $1,500
- It's possible to pay as low as $2,500 in labor to do your framing

Real estate investing is like any other business. Remember that your success will depend on your local market and how the housing sector is doing as a whole. In a slow market, you may find that buying properties to rehab and sell is just not realistic, but once the housing market heats up, you may find that it becomes much more feasible.

As of this writing, the market is very cold and showing signs of a major cooling. Rates are between 6% and 7% for people with excellent or above average credit. Of course those rates won't stay this low forever. Some people prefer rentals, others like the idea of fixers. When the market turns down, foreclosures are always back in fashion.

Watch the market, get informed and don't be afraid to make a move once you've read several books on investing and you trust that the market is moving forward, not stagnating.

A house is made of walls and beams; a home is built with love and dreams!

MENSELECT.COM
FOOL'S GOLD

The American experiment has now grown into a beacon of hope – a place millions aspire to call home. Let us not forget how lucky we are that the freedom to become anything we desire has a name: The United States of America.

Glenn Gary

Many people, particularly wives and young adults, don't have much interest in the stock market or in investing in a company before it goes public. Of course there are more and more women entering the field of stock investing, but the following stories are designed for my readers to learn more about how to protect themselves from losing money on the next great investment opportunity. Whether you're a stay at home domestic engineer, a young adult about to enter college, or a wife who is not running the finances and is listening to her husband talk about the stock market or investing in a company, or maybe you're the next Carly Fiorina (former CEO of Hewlett-Packard), anything is possible with a bit of solid knowledge.

One day that I will always remember for its incredible absurdity was when Ronald, Jason, and Eric rode into my office with a half-baked idea that menselect.com was going to replace Nordstrom as the place men would go to purchase shoes, ties, and shirts. I was astonished to learn that Ronald was one of the founding partners of Anderson Consulting and a managing director of Arthur Anderson Worldwide. With that background, I would have expected much more common sense. Jason had stints with PepsiCo and Carter

Hawley Hale, and he was a division president for Baxter Healthcare & Caremark International. Ronald, CEO of this soon-to-be online retail clothing empire, was a senior manager with Ernst & Young. What in the world were four very bright individuals doing in my conference room, attempting to convince me that somehow men would want to buy their clothes on the Internet and that department stores were going to go out of business as a result? As I reviewed their business plan, the only thing that impressed me was the group's collective resume.

"So gentleman," I asked them, "before we start our meeting let me ask you how much money you have raised to date." I was hoping to hear that these guys did the honorable thing and ponied up the money from their savings or tapped into the equity in their homes. I was, of course, dead wrong.

Ronald, the CEO replied gleefully, "Well, we have raised just over $3.6 million from friends and family." I just about spit up my mocha. Even worse, as I scanned my conference table all I could see were big smug smiles and grins from ear to ear. They were darn proud of this tidbit of information. I suddenly felt a sick feeling in my stomach. I no longer wanted to talk with these guys. Their next statement just about put me over the edge. "Wow gentleman. That's a heck of a lot of money to raise from your group of friends and family. Since you have no current revenue to speak of, what do you feel the company is worth at this stage of the game?" Jason replied, "We think the company is worth $60 million."

After hearing that insane statement, it was all that I could do to restrain myself from throwing these lunatics out of my office. It made me sick to think that they would never be able to pay their friends and family back, along with the knowledge that several people probably lost their entire life's savings because this circus had convinced them that men hated going to the mall. It didn't seem to dawn on them that not only were they taking this startup down a road to Chapter 11 bankruptcy quicker then a falling Enron executive, but they were morally bankrupt as well.

I decided to respond to their plan with the following: "You know guys, I have a real problem with your business model. It's true that women love to shop, in fact I think it's therapeutic for woman to go shopping. It's their time to be with friends and of course if they're in a bad mood or feeling down, well then sometimes they may really need a trip to the mall." I gave the following example about myself. "I may be a bit different from most men in the sense that I buy custom shirts to wear with my suits and I like getting them made for me because they fit better. I can pick my colors and styles, and they're unique. I get my initials monogrammed, and so on. Certainly, most men hate to shop. But there is no way that most men can buy their clothes without trying them on. As much as we may not see the mall as a good place to gossip with our friends and shop, how do you expect fashion-challenged men to just click their way to a shoe?" I tried to rationalize with this group. "Why would anyone want to pick expensive clothes off of some tiny little picture on a fuzzy computer screen? How does that make sense?"

Their mission statement was "to become the dominant global retail service provider (RSP) in the apparel industry by leveraging Internet technology." Wow! That's a mouthful. I think the only thing this group was going to dominate was the crisis center hotline for help in repairing the broken family relationships after the loss of all of the money that they had bamboozled from their friends and family. It's now 2008, and when I went to the mall a few weeks back, it was slammed wall to wall with people. Seems some things never change. Some people think that their glossy resumes and slick business plan can hide the impossible. E-commerce in the clothing industry will never drive malls out of business.

In many situations, men choose to lead with their ego; women choose to lead with their emotions, with their heart. This plays out much like the following:

Lunch with the average "alpha male" could consist of him telling you what he knows, making sure his expertise is front and center to the exclusion of your ideas or anything about you. The alpha male's ego is commanding your full attention.

Lunch with a woman may involve a more evolved conversation about you, how you're doing, your kids, life etc. In short, it most likely won't feel as though you have been taken to the woodshed for a lecture.

Maybe you can become the exception to these rules....

Glenn Gary

O nce again the winds of change swept my way. The dot com economy was about to take over. In 1997, if you didn't work for a new dot com startup, most likely you knew someone who did. Like most people, I was looking to stake my claim in the Internet gold rush. Of course the road I would take would be much different from the roads of others.

I planned to be in charge of my new career. I would attack this reinvention by quickly gained new skills. Before I could begin what would eventually become my five year odyssey into investment banking, consulting, and advising well over 140 high tech, biotech, wireless, pharmaceutical, internet and food and beverage startups and running my own boutique mergers and acquisitions firm, I knew that I needed a technical background in securities.

I immediately threw myself into hitting the books and studying for my Series 7 securities license. It took months of intense study, but ultimately I possessed extensive knowledge of how the stock market worked, common and preferred stock, private placements, IPO's, valuations etc. Armed with this new knowledge, I was fortunate to meet one of my early investment banking mentors. I didn't know it at the time, but meeting Jack would give me a crash course in the IPO game and, more importantly, the tricks, double dealing and unfortunately the crimes that people commit in order to chase the almighty American dollar. Unfortunately for Jack, he would end up as his own worst enemy.

Jack and I had gone to high school together, but our roads took vastly different courses after that. After high school, I was busy running my company and trying to keep a successful business going. Jack would go on to UCLA and an Economics degree. Unfortunately, he developed a few vices along the way that would eventually be his downfall, but before that, he was the most talented investment banker that I had ever met. To watch him on the phone browbeating and bullying CEOs who had come to him seeking capital was truly amazing. To watch him unwind a CFO was an education for me. Picture him for a moment: John Belushi-like in appearance, well over 220 pounds, with a rapid-fire speech delivery that made him seem like a large, lurking bull in a china shop. Now, dress all of that up in a custom shirt, slap on some cuff links, a silk tie, and put a monogram on the shirt. Add some suspenders and you have a large version of Gordon Gecko on speed. That was Jack, a big, hulking, tor-tured, and extremely talented man of corporate finance. I would learn more from him in one year than most people could have learned in ten years.

When our two roads crossed again, he was the managing director of corporate finance for the small tier 3 firm, Waldron & Co. in Newport Beach. One of my clients from my small phone distribution and wireless company was an emerging growth company based in Orange County, shopping.com. I was looking to get out of the wireless business, and dot coms and early-stage IPO's were becoming all the rage. My experience with shopping.com was a shining example of how rich you could become with a bit of hype and excellent timing. Of course, behind the scenes of any successful IPO is someone who makes the magic fly, and in this case, the master puppeteer was Jack. As I walked into the corporate offices of shopping.com to deliver some of my high-tech wireless devices to the founder and CEO, it was like walking onto a college campus. Everyone in this new e-commerce startup seemed to be under the age of 25, everyone except for Bob McNaulty. Bob and Jack made for an interesting and somewhat unlikely duo. It was a marriage of convenience. Bob was in his sixties: grumpy, pushy, and manipulative, from a business standpoint, and of course a good salesman for the power of the Internet and the new emerging e-commerce generation.

Back in the late '90's, these two preached the Internet gospel. We were all to believe that with the advent of the Internet, consumers would no longer want to get in their car to fetch an item from a crowded mall. Instead we would all just jump online, point our browser over to shopping.com and voila, click and purchase to our heart's content.

This thinking made many investors very wealthy, but in the end it was foolhardy at best. Shopping.com went public at $9 a share in late 1997 and set out to raise $12 million with an offering of 1.3 million shares of common stock. It was barely a whimper in comparison to the big payday of Wall Street IPO's; we weren't talking Goldman Sachs or Bear Sterns, but it was still a nice shot. The company had accumulated $1.3 million in losses by July of 1997. By the end of that year, they had almost 50 employees. Like many dot coms they had a bunch of young people on the payroll (doing who knows what), but it seemed like overkill to me upon my visit to their corporate office. They were competing with the likes of other huge money losers like amazon.com, NetGrocer, and iMall.

Shopping.com was formed in February 1996 and began selling products on its web site in July of 1997. Not a very long track record but, hey, this was the Internet gold rush during which people were hyping anything with a ".com" attached to its name. Shopping.com gained a little bit more notoriety than other dot coms due to the fact that Idealab founder Bill Gross was chairman of the board. However, as the company could not qualify for listing on NASDAQ, it had to start life off on the OTC Electronic Bulletin Board under the symbol IBUY. It was basically the minor leagues.

Jack's undoing was sad to watch. From my perspective, the previous year had been a good one. He made almost half a million dollars taking shopping.com public, bought himself a $90,000 Mercedes and a new home on a golf course, and got married. A year later, it was all over. His recently developed addiction to cocaine was too powerful. Eventually, it shattered his marriage; he lost the car, his house and his credit. His losses were not solely economic; he also lost his self-respect and his dignity. I saw him on many occasions, strung out on rock cocaine and speed, and it was an ugly sight. No amount of money, success, or material possession can mask a deeper problem. Addiction was taking his life away. The last time I heard from Jack, he was living with his mother in Nevada. That's a pretty big fall from where he had been. I fear that he too will travel down the same road as John Belushi. To see such a talent wasted is truly sad. Shopping.com was eventually sold for $240 million dollars, and Bob McNaulty walked away with more than $60 million. The company is still on the Internet today under new owners.

The stock market is much like the real estate market in that it constantly shifts with ups and downs and major corrections from time to time that can possible wipe someone out financially. Certainly many people have made their fortune by investing in a company before it goes public. But often, many have lost their entire life savings. Raising your consciousness and living an enlightened existence requires that you become students of these and or other financial vehicles. Securing your financial future through one or both of these vehicles is a way that may free you to ultimately discover your true purpose in life and have the financial resources at your disposal to take action on that purpose. But you must become a student of either discipline. Higher living will mandate that you seek out new ways of securing your future, but you must be hungry for the knowledge. The dot coms made people millions but also wiped other people out financially. Though we may never see this exact dot com bubble again, somewhere in your future the stock market will be caught up in another wild frenzy, and everyone you know may want to go along for the ride.

Don't Get Scammed on an Investment Opportunity: A Checklist

■ You may be shown slick, glossy and very expensive marketing brochures, offering memorandums and private placement stock offerings, but does the company have something as small as a 411 business listing? You would be amazed at how many don't. It's a clear sign that they are not looking at the details and probably never plan to operate from a legitimate and permanent business address. Obviously, most scam artists move around quite a bit in every facet of their personal and professional life.

■ Find out if they are incorporated with the state in which they operate.

■ Ask for a list of 20 other investors, including names, phone numbers, etc. If no list can be provided, it is a clear sign that bad news is being kept from new investors. Getting a list of the 20 is not an instant stamp of approval; it just may mean that there are 20 other gullible, naive investors who did not do their homework.

■ Find out how much capital the company has raised, and what they have done with it. If the company reps behave arrogantly (and many of them will), do not fall into the trap. Whenever I ran across an arrogant start-up company that gave me the attitude that investors were "lucky" to be getting in, I got out... and fast!

■ Look up the background on the principals.

■ Visit their offices, see how they are spending their money; is it furnished with expensive items? Is it a ghost town? Would you run the place the way they do?

■ Look at résumés and bios of the principals. Are they in the office full time, or, like many start-ups, are they just lending their name to the venture for a little bit of the stock/equity etc?

■ Find out the price of the stock. Is it $2.00 per share in a private placement or .50 cents per share? More importantly, what is their current valuation? Are they saying that it's $20 million and they're pre-revenue, or a much more realistic $3 million with a little bit of revenue?

■ Find out if they are "patent pending," like most startups, or if they indeed have a United States Patent. There is a big difference. Anyone can file and call themselves patent pending; it's a whole new ball game when they have a patent.

■ Find out if they have a real product or are raising money so that you, and all the other investors, can pay for it. Put another way, does the founder and CEO have his own money in the venture, and is he willing to prove it? I can't tell you how many CEO's I have sat down with who claimed to have put over a million dollars of their own money into the venture. You can tell if you just dig hard enough whether or not there is a million dollars invested in the venture.

■ Can you buy stock in a privately held company at $2.00 per share and someday, when it goes public, watch it rocket up to $30 per share and become rich? Yes. Plenty of people have done just that, but it's a long shot. It had better be one very special company with an awesome piece of new technology, and it would require some very good, ethical people to run it. It can be done, but more often than not, people are not savvy about what they are looking at, and they fall victim to the many con-artists who are morally bankrupt, and who, at the end of they day, sometimes drive their investors to bankruptcy as well.

IDENTITY THEFT

It's estimated that 10 million Americans are victims of identity theft each year.

I first learned of the infamous Abraham Abdallah as I sat in my doctor's office of all places. It's amazing how much you can learn when you are surrounded by sick people!

Identity theft is now getting lots of press. Even our U.S. Congress finally woke up and started the legislative process in 2005 to address this crime now that it affects most Americans regardless of income, social standing, or location. But, let's roll back the clock a few years ago as we take a look at famous celebrities who were high-profile identity theft victims and examine how the theft methods used then are still being used against the rest of us who actually work for a living. Now that it's faster for the Internet enabled identity thief to conduct his research and piece together your confidential profile, identity theft has become a huge national crisis. If you don't think it can hurt you, you're wrong. Identity theft can absolutely destroy all that you have worked so hard for.

More and more people know of loved ones who have had personal information exposed or abused through no fault of their own. But here's a question: what do you have in common with the following celebrities?

Oprah
Tiger Woods
Warren Buffett
Mel Gibson
Ross Perot

Steven Spielberg
Martha Stewart
Ted Turner
Paris Hilton
Lindsay Lohan
Christina Aguilera

And up to 100 others who were targeted by just two very industrious identity thieves.

Answer: They were all victims of identity theft.

Meet Identity Thief #1:

Abraham Abdallah, a 32-year-old high school dropout at the time of his arrest in 2001.

Court papers say Abdallah had a dog-eared copy of a Forbes "400 Richest" article, with notations of social security numbers, home addresses and birth dates of 200 chief executives, celebrities and tycoons. They say he also had more than 400 stolen credit card numbers, one belonging to a federal prosecutor. Posing as his victims, he obtained social security numbers, credit card numbers and all vital financial records. With this information, he contacted their banks and brokerage firms. Couriers and prostitutes all across New York City were used to deliver expensive items bought with the victims' credit cards and accounts at brokerage houses such as Goldman Sachs, Bear Stearns and Merrill Lynch. Like most victims even today, Turner and Spielberg were unaware their identities may have been stolen. The scheme started to unravel when Merrill Lynch executives got suspicious about an e-mail request to transfer $10 million from an account belonging to Thomas Siebel, founder of Siebel Systems.

Meet Identity Thief #2:

James Rinaldo Jackson, among other things, a Steven Spielberg fanatic.

Such a fanatic, in fact, that for an entire year in the mid-1990s, he knew everything Spielberg purchased on his American Express card. Everything Jackson learned about Spielberg, he learned while in prison, much of it using a cell phone supplied by a family member. Just a few calls while in the care of the federal prison system, and Jackson scored all sorts of data on Spielberg and about 100 other Hollywood types.

Here's how you can protect your identity:

■ Release only your social security number (SSN) information to only those few legitimate entities which really require it for your benefit.

■ Determine how those entities safeguard your personal information and under what exact circumstances will they release it to third parties without your consent.

■ Do not provide personal information to telemarketers, especially not credit card numbers, PIN #'s, social security number, mother's maiden name, or your date of birth.

■ Establish rigorous passwords for accessing your banking, credit card, and utility accounts by using upper/lower case/numeric combinations. Change these passwords every three months.

■ For online shopping, use a dedicated credit card with online statement access and a low limit. For extra protection, either have your account number changed or take advantage of the cards which utilize a "temporary" account number.

■ Limit your credit card purchases, especially in restaurants. You slap down your credit card and away it goes with the waiter or waitress; most of them are very hard working people, but all it takes is one bad one to wipe you out. I try to use cash whenever possible. Unfortunately we did not have to worry about this as much 20 years ago as we do today.

■ Try to pay cash at the gas pump, too. Thieves have come up with devices so that after you have used your credit card at the pump and driven away, they can stick this device in and access your info.

■ Every American should own a paper shredder. One of the easiest ways thieves have is to simply go through your trash and access your receipts and statements, so it's absolutely vital that you shred everything.

■ Many people don't think about all of those credit card offers they receive each month. I must get at least 20 of them monthly. It's critical that you shred the bottom part with your name and the application form; this is another way thieves can get credit cards in your name.

■ You can also put fraud alerts on your credit file, which gives you another means of protection.

If you are the victim it can take hundreds of hours in letter writing and phone calls to get your identity back. You must protect your identity so that you don't lose your entire life savings and all that you worked for; you must also secure your future through homeownership and/or investment in stocks. Navigating through this hyper tech world that we now live in requires that we become very savvy about almost every move we make, including something as mundane as paying for dinner with a credit card. We live in a world that demands that we raise our consciousness about these issues or suffer greatly. My professional contact with large numbers of people has given me a perspective that allows me to see that much of the pain that we experience is either self-induced or comes from a lack of knowledge.

We move away from finances to explore our health in Part 4. It has been said that without our health, we cannot enjoy our wealth. Going the extra mile and learning advanced forms of health detection will be our focus. Moreover, looking inside the body to see what is really happening will be our primary focus. Most people realize that living without regular exercise and healthy eating is a one way ticket to greater suffering in our lives as we begin to age. As the following chapters have you looking inside your body and really understanding what is taking place, you will dramatically increase the length and quality of your life.

"It's not enough to have lived. We should determine to live for something. May I suggest that it be creating joy for others, sharing what we have for the betterment of all, bringing hope to the lost and love to the lonely." Only you will be able to discover, realize, develop and actualize your uniqueness. And when you do, it's your duty to then "give it away."

Part 4

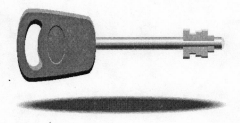

Developing a Greater Health Consciousness

DEPRESSION: A STATE OF MIND THAT YOU CONTROL

Is being fully aware a move towards a state of active cognition? In every day life, self-actualization can be seen in, for example, your decision to drink bottled water instead of tap water. Then, you go a step further and research bottled water. Why? Because you're more conscious of everything that you do than your average person. But you now experience another dilemma. You know that in some areas of the country, bottled water is worse than tap. Once you have arrived at this point, you are fully conscious, although now you must decide which kind of water to drink, quite a quandary to be sure.

Glenn Gary

D epression is often very hard to control, but I would argue that you do have some control over it. Sometimes you make a conscious decision to stay in this unproductive, crippling state; others may not be so aware and conscious. Much of our depression is self-induced; at other times it sets in through no fault of our own. For instance the months of depression that followed my discovery of my mother's body were not experienced by choice. However, higher living dictates that you become aware of self-induced depression and why you are choosing to be stuck in neutral, waiting for someone else to kick your life into gear. You must make the decision to leave that relationship, to quit that depressing dead end job, or even better, alter your state of mind by physically getting off the couch and heading to the gym, running so that endorphins are released and you alter your state of mind completely.

I would suggest that when we do not take action in our lives, this lack of action leads to a greater, prolonged, self-induced state of depression, which just continues to make the situation even worse. As we seek and gain greater awareness of ourselves, as we begin the journey towards self-actualization, we learn that our states of mind are within our control. I am not suggesting that as you suffer through a miserable marriage or fight obesity, you are not experiencing pain and frustration. However, even more difficult is a life of quiet desperation in which you cease to take daily action to change your circumstances.

Moving out of that crummy apartment, disengaging from toxic friends, whatever your reality is that you want to manifest, you can do so once you understand that depression and prolonged frustration is to a great degree your choice. The key is that we will always be upset and frustrated by events in our lives; higher living dictates that you take action. Those who don't take action suffer from their miserable set of circumstances by choice. This situation is one that I found myself to be in many times until I became more aware of these negative actions. At the end of the day, taking action is that simple and that straightforward. Financial success, fancy cars, nice homes, excellent relationships, rewarding careers — these achievements are all examples of healthy choices made over a consistent period of time, choices that separate those living a life of abundance from those constantly unhappy. Turning your back on depression is a conscious decision.

My walk in life has been challenged by several chapters of depression. For months after my car accident, mourning Craig's death left me on the couch, unable to live a life. Fortunately I was only 17 and had the time and youthful energy to recognize this dangerous trap and move past it. I had a poor role model, though; my father slumped into his TV chair every night, locked in a dark room, choosing to not live. At 20, after my mother's death, once again depression was choking the life right out of me. Week after week I was losing clients and my business, but when I lost my home, I finally picked up a phone and reached for helped.

One of the best things I ever did was to enter into weekly counseling during this difficult time. Counselors, psychologists and therapists are wonderful, compassionate people who can help you to better understand yourself. Through this process you will gain the clarity and awareness needed to make dramatic changes in your life.

In my late twenties, stuck in a rut, depression had me in a chokehold for a third time, but I was now much more adept at recognizing the signs and could fight my way out of the darkness. Ultimately your mental health is in your hands: you can choose to use Prozac and Zoloft and become addicted to drugs, in the process, living an unconscious life, or you can simply learn to seek greater self-awareness and "treat yourself" without drugs, seek new and better friends, find a life coach, seek counseling and start to become the architect of the life that you want to live. In the end, it's always your choice.

A man spends the first half of his life learning habits that shorten the other half.

Author Unknown

NOTE: For more severe cases of depression, it is critical to be evaluated by a mental health professional. If you are suffering from severe and prolonged depression you are not alone. A Harvard Medical School study found depression affects roughly 6.6 percent of American adults in a given year, and 16.2 percent of American adults in a lifetime. According to another survey, nearly 15 million Americans suffer from depression each year due to a chemical imbalance in the brain. The college-aged group accounts for much of that number, according to WebMD. In a survey of 17,000 college students conducted by the National College Health Assessment, 25 percent of students reported they "felt so depressed it was difficult to function" three to eight times during the previous year. In the same survey, 18 percent said depression was one of their top physical/mental ailments.

HOW HEALTHY IS YOUR HEART?

The power to change the course of our lives is within all of us; sadly many people choose to live a life ignoring the signs that change must be imminent in order to avoid greater pain.

Glenn Gary

On September 11th, 2003 we were once again hit with great sadness when John Ritter died of a congenital heart problem. It is my view that one cannot write a comprehensive book covering everything from your finances to your health without discussing one of our most vital organs, the heart. Most people only think of their hearts when they have been broken. I submit that if you don't think of your heart today, it might lead to your early exit from the reality that is your life.

Sadly, John Ritter was fully aware of his heart condition. His father had died from heart problems some thirty years earlier. Ironically John died in the same hospital in which he was born fifty four years earlier. Ritter had gone through the efforts to have a full body scan at the age of fifty two, but doctors failed to detect the enlargement of Ritter's aorta. The exact cause of John Ritter's death is an aortic dissection caused by a previously undiagnosed congenital heart defect.

With the recent announcement in November of 2007 of Philips super high-resolution 256-slice CT scanner which shows from the inside the heart in magnificent 3D images, there is no longer any excuse to not see and fully understand what is happening within your body and specifically your heart. As of this writing, the CT scan will cost you just under $2,000.

As has been the theme of this book, it is my view that we cannot live to our fullest potential if we are deficient in some major part of our lives. A lack of awareness of just how healthy our hearts really are, the one organ that plays one of the most vital roles in keeping you alive each day, is in itself a true crime. Too many people die each year from heart disease while still in their mid-fifties, much like John Ritter.

So the following stories and essays will seek to illuminate one of the most vital parts of living your greatest life: taking the necessary steps towards achieving an excellent state and higher awareness of your health. As you make these radical changes to your health, you can also be an instrument of greater health in the lives of those around you.

HOW HEALTHY IS YOUR MAN?

*Your careful examination of all parts of your life,
from the ingredients of food you eat to the people
you allow into your life and the information that
you choose to take in and adopt will be the critical,
determining factor in the levels of success that you
attain. Success in not an accident, but the clever
pursuit of a goal from a person who is committed to
reaching it.*

Glenn Gary

For anyone who has a significant man in his or her life – husbands, dads, brothers, or uncles, the following story may resonate. Recently I went through a prostate cancer scare. As I was only 38 years old at the time, it was a complete surprise to me. My sincere hope is that this experience will help you encourage the man in your life to get screened for prostate cancer. If cancer is caught early, his life can be saved.

I had just gotten a routine blood test that screened for everything, cholesterol and all the other stuff—a test I had been putting off for many years. About a week later, my doctor called me in a panic to say that my cholesterol level was good, but my PSA level was 7.0. I didn't even know what a PSA was until that fateful day. It stands for prostate specific antigen. If it's above 4.0 then doctors start to get pretty worried.

My regular doctor referred me to a urologist. Of course that day I came home and jumped on webmd.com and started to panic. One minute you're fine and the next you're freaking out that you may have cancer; the worst part is, you don't even know what prostate cancer is. The prostate is a small gland, the size of a walnut, located around the urethra. It manufactures part of the fluid that makes up the semen that carries the sperm to its ultimate destination. I was told by three doctors that every male who lives long enough will develop prostate cancer.

The good news is that in this advanced Internet age, you can quickly rise to the level of diligence and find out too much information. My research allowed me to understand that musician Frank Zappa died of prostate cancer at just 52. The irony that Zappa used to live one block from my home in the early seventies has not been lost on me. Though I was not a fan of his music, it's wrong for anyone to die at 52. Chances are that had Zappa gotten a PSA blood test in his mid or early forties, he most likely would have survived.

In addition, I also learned that TV actor Bill Bixby (The Incredible Hulk) died from this cancer at 59. John Kerry, Gen. Norman Schwarzkopf, former FBI Director Robert Mueller, former Sen. Bob Dole, former Gen. Colin Powell, media tycoon Rupert Murdoch, Dodgers manager Joe Torre, and former New York Mayor Rudolph Giuliani have all been recently diagnosed with prostate cancer.

As it turns out, the longer a man lives the greater the chances that he will develop prostate cancer. Longevity has its hazards. But many oldsters, who have a slow-growing prostate cancer, usually die of something else. Prostate cancer usually does not strike men until their 50's, but not in my case. In fact I had to torture myself by asking this dumb question, "So doc, what's the youngest person you have had in your office and diagnosed with prostate cancer?" My urologist's answer was 42!

Hence, it's critical if your man is approaching 40 or above, you must encourage him to get this life saving test.

"If a man lives long enough, it's very likely that there will be some prostate cancer found."

Dr. Emily Senay, CBS News

Here are the raw facts that every man approaching 40 needs to know.

About 190,000 cases of prostate cancer are diagnosed in the United States every year, and about 30,000 men died of the disease in 2002, according to American Cancer Society statistics. It is the most common cancer in American men and their second-leading cause of cancer death after lung cancer.

Prostate cancer is the third deadliest cancer for Americans. Lung, breast and colorectal cancers kill more people overall. An American man has a 30 percent chance of getting prostate cancer, but only a 3 percent risk of dying from it, according to the Mayo clinic.

Black men, such as Collin Powell, have the highest rates of prostate cancer, and while death rates have been in decline for a decade, the rate is still twice as high for blacks as for whites.

This incident started me down the road of exploring other diseases in my own family history. It turns out my mother's mom, my grandmother, died from colon cancer, in my mind one of the worst and most uncomfortable cancers you could get. I now found myself asking all the guys at my tennis club about their own health. Here's what I found out in just one week. Several of the men on my tennis ladder knew of someone in their family with prostate cancer. This led them to have themselves and their wives checked with a routine colonoscopy. This is a test that allows your doctor to look at the interior lining of your large intestine (rectum and colon) through a thin, flexible viewing instrument called a colonoscope. A colonoscopy helps detect ulcers, polyps, tumors, and areas of inflammation or bleeding. During a colonoscopy, tissue samples can be collected and abnormal growths can be removed. Colonoscopy can also be used as a screening test to identify and remove pre-cancerous and cancerous growths in the colon or rectum. One of the guys that I talked to had a wife who had pre-cancerous polyps removed; she was only in her mid 30's. You too need to get these tests done, or you could have issues building inside of you for many years that go undetected, a very scary thought for me as a professional speaker who would like to still be giving keynotes when I am 70.

After my first visit with my urologist I had a digital rectal exam (DRE) done, which suffice to say was not fun. I did not enjoy having a person with a rubber glove on poke around inside of me, but it lasted just 30 seconds and was very important. The doctor told me that because everything seemed fine, I probably had a false positive on my PSA test, which is common. The DRE is important because if you have advanced stages of prostate cancer the doctor can actually feel it inside the prostate during the DRE exam. A week later I went back for another PSA test, and it came back 4.4. Still not good. Now it was time for the biopsy, where they go inside and take tissue samples for analysis; after this, you really know whether you have prostate cancer.

The biopsy was very uncomfortable mentally and physically, but it lasted only 20 minutes and was done inside the doctor's office. My urologist happened to be the same age as me and a veteran of hundreds of prostate removal operations. I went in on a Friday morning and spent the rest of the day and weekend in bed. They put me on antibiotics for two days and I had a bit of nausea, but it was worth finding out whether I had cancer. The weekend was very hard to get through due to the fact that physically it felt as though my internal plumbing had been assaulted. Without getting too far into the ugly details, I will say there was some blood to deal with in addition to the nausea, but it cleared up after 3 days. Besides having to stay in bed for a few days of rest, the worst part was the anxiety over whether I had cancer. Suddenly life had changed and I was now aware of how fragile the body can be. As I like to remind people during my keynotes, *you're not wealthy unless you're healthy!*

My prostate cancer scare lasted almost a full month. I can't begin to tell you about how much anxiety built up inside of me during this time. In the end I came away from the ordeal with more appreciation for my own health and the health of others. I truly believe lives can be saved, and you're the one who can save those lives by making people around you aware of the need for screening.

A SAILOR'S LAST RUN

*Transcending your reality and escaping the impris-
onment of your current state of despair is within
you. The only prerequisite asked of you is that you
identify and follow a greater purpose for your life
than the one that you currently hold.*

Glenn Gary

I had considered going to work for Ed. The position was in sales and marketing, which implied that I would be working for myself, but somehow I knew that if I worked for Ed, I would actually be working for him and not for myself, which was an uncomfortable thought. Ed had a very stern and direct way about him. He was from the East Coast, and prior to his acquiring this small building services company he was an accountant. I was coming off of a position at a company with annual sales of nearly $100 million a year. Ed's company was lucky if it grossed $1.5 million a year. In business, size does matter, and I was not comfortable with the idea of such a small company. Ed wanted to meet and thought that a sailing trip off the coast of Santa Monica might do the trick. Though I was not an avid sailor, I figured I could learn a lot about a man if I spent the day sailing with him. It turned out I was right.

It was a warm September day, perfect for sailing. Ed had a 40 footer docked near his home, obviously his pride and joy. We had a great day of sailing, but after many hours of discussion, it was clear that Ed would be running a tight and stern ship, so to speak, and that probably was not going to be a good fit for me as I needed a lot more autonomy in my sales career. This was in addition to the fact that his company was just too small to work with.

Though I decided not to work for Ed, I did the next best thing and referred my friend Tom to him, which turned out to be a great move for both of them. They went on to develop a close and long-running business relationship from which both were able to prosper. Like many things in business, and in life, the right situation and the right people are often all you need to be successful. Tom and Ed collaborated for several years, and I kept in touch with both of them from time to time. That being said, it was still a shock to receive Tom's call one day out of the blue.

"Glenn, hey, it's Tom Dudley."

"Tom, hey man, good to hear from you. How are you and Ed doing?" I figured he had good news, as the last time I had spoken with him, he had mentioned that the business had doubled over the past year.

"Not very well. I am afraid that Ed died yesterday. I wanted to call and let you know that his funeral service will be held in Beverly Hills."

I was stunned of course and figured that something was not right, as Ed was in his early fifties. I had thought he was in pretty good shape for his age.

"Tom, he was so young! What happened?"

"Well believe it or not, he was at the gym running on the treadmill, and he just suddenly had a heart attack and died right there on the spot."

I couldn't believe what I was hearing. Of all things to happen when he was doing what's good for the body. I heard that he only recently had begun to exercise. Obviously he would have died whether he was on a treadmill or sleeping.

I found it difficult to see his wife and family at the service as we all gathered to reflect on his life. Ed was a difficult man to work with, but I felt sad thinking back on that late summer day when we were sailing together. On that day he had everything that he needed: a successful small business and the opportunity to do what he wanted to do. He was living the life of a small and successful entrepreneur.

People come in and out of our lives at a moment's notice. When we spend time with a person, we never think that it may be the last time with that person. But we must remember the people with whom we connect in this life and never take a moment with them for granted. In some cases that moment will come and go, and we may feel deep regret for the things that we said or did not do.

I do not regret my decision to not work with Ed. Rather, I had given him someone better suited for his personality. Sure enough it worked and they built an even better company together. In some small way I made a contribution to his life by bringing him and Tom together. For that, I was happy. I also kept in touch with his wife, and I gave her advice at her request about how to value the company now that Ed was gone. She was set on selling. Sure enough, I knew who the buyer would be, as I knew that Tom would be the one to carry the torch forward for Ed's company. In looking back, I prefer to remember Ed on that great sailing trip one beautiful sunny day.

This underscores the need to take control of our health in our thirties and forties so that we can prevent problems like Ed's from developing in our fifties. Regardless of your age, today is the day when you can decide to take control of your health, get the proper heart scans done so that you know what's going on inside your body, and take the necessary steps to ensure that your walk through life is a long and joyous one.

WHAT YOUR DOG CAN TEACH YOU ABOUT YOUR HEALTH

D ogs are often used to provide therapy in hospice settings and nursing homes, and they also serve as companions to the disabled. Pet ownership in the golden years has a positive effect on a senior's physical and emotional well-being, according to the *Journal of American Geriatrics Society*. Studies have also revealed that people on Medicaid or Medicare who own a pet make fewer visits to the doctor. Hospitals and nursing homes have begun taking down the "No Dogs Allowed" from their doors after realizing the healing effects of dogs. The unconditional acceptance and love a dog gives to its owners positively impacts their owner's emotional health, particularly among the elderly. Some of these benefits include:

- Bringing joy and laughter to daily life, which in later years is often uneventful
- Giving the person something to do, talk about and think about, other than him or herself
- Providing a source of touch and affiliation
- Boosting self-confidence and self-esteem
- Promoting communication between elderly residents and neighbors
- Helping ease newcomers with transitions and meeting new friends
- Raising overall morale
- Encouraging exercise and activity
- Helping people cope with illness, loss and depression.
- Reducing stress levels

Pets Keep Hearts Healthy

Having a dog as a companion could add years to your life; two studies have shown that owning a dog played a significant role on survival rates in heart attack victims. In one study, patients who were admitted to the hospital for heart attacks were evaluated for one year. Researchers discovered that the patients who were alive one year after the heart attack were more likely to own a dog. To emphasize this point, another study on psychological factors contributing to the recovery rates for heart-disease patients ranked pet ownership on top in terms of determining the patient's likelihood of long-term survival. Studies have also shown how the calming and soothing presence of dogs helps with keeping blood pressure levels in the healthy range. In one study, the State University of New York at Buffalo conducted a study involving 24 stockbrokers taking medication for high blood pressure. The researchers found that adding a dog or cat to the stock brokers' lives helped stabilize and reduce their stress levels. It certainly works for me!

WHAT WOMEN DON'T KNOW MAY KILL THEM

As we live life, we should be reminded of the power that we have to achieve greatness in spite of severe neglect in our young lives. It's the human spirit within us that has conquered overwhelming odds to survive, thrive and come back to live another day. Bad experiences are lessons, and we can use them to become fully powerful or we can self-destruct. In the end, it's always our choice.

Glenn Gary

The sad fact is that my mother did not have to die at the age of 51. In fact she should still be alive today, and the mere fact that I cannot take her out to a nice dinner and share my life with her is another reminder of how women across America are dying way before their time due to strokes, cancer and heart disease. Consider these sobering facts:

Heart disease is responsible for more deaths in women than all forms of cancer combined. Heart disease is the most significant health concern for women in the United States today, responsible for nearly 489,000 deaths each year.

The common belief that heart disease affects mostly men is a dangerous myth. In reality, more women than men die of heart disease in the United States each year. But according to the American Heart Association, only 13 percent of women know that heart disease is a major threat to their health.

Nearly 163,000 people in the United States die of strokes each year, and almost two-thirds of them are women.

Stroke is not only the No. 3 killer of women, but it also is one of the leading causes of disability in America.

Smoking and uncontrolled high blood pressure are important risk factors for stroke. Although stroke is highly preventable, certain risk factors such as family history, age, sex and race cannot be controlled. Even if you're at increased risk of stroke, you can still take steps to prevent it:

1) *Don't smoke.*

2) *Control your blood pressure.*

3) *Lower your cholesterol.*

4) *Limit saturated fats.*

5) *Exercise regularly.*

6) *Get a 256- Slice CT Scan after you turn 40;*
   it could save your life!

The next time you put off running, going to the gym, eating healthy foods, or quitting your smoking habit, think about the loved ones that you may leave behind. Think about your husband and your kids and the people who love you. Use that as motivation for getting on a treadmill for 30 minutes three times a week. Heck if you have to, carry a picture of your kids, your family or your husband with you and stick it on the treadmill for the 30 minutes that you're running. Had my mother started those activities in her thirties she most likely would not have died at 51. Don't leave behind children and family simply because you were too tired to exercise; your life depends on it! Your kids should be taking you to dinner, not visiting you at the cemetery.

> *I had a life with options but frequently lived as if I*
> *had none. The sad result of my not having exercised*
> *my choices is that my memory of myself is not of the*
> *woman I believe I am.*
>
> *-Liv Ullmann*

ACTION STEPS FOR GREATER HEALTH

I am just not a big fan of vegetables, and I bet your family struggles with this problem too. We know from watching our kids hide veggies under the mashed potatoes that they don't like them either. I am going to share with you my greatest secret to solving this problem. You have probably heard about it, but most people who have don't take any action on it.

Before I reveal my secret, let me share with you another of my food issues: my addictions to a certain drink that was tearing up my insides. From 1998 through 2001 I was pretty stressed out in the intense game of investment banking. These were the go-go days of the dot com gold rush, and my morning routine was simple. I would start each day before getting to my office with a venti mocha from Starbucks. Most of us know that's a lot of coffee.

All of this caffeine was reducing my appetite, so of course I did not eat until way past 3 pm. Around that hour, my body would be coming off the caffeine high and starting to crash, so I would do what any other coffee addict would do: head back to Starbucks for another venti. Now that's pretty far from the breakfast of champions, and by dinner time, my body was a mess.

After a few years of this nonsense, I finally realized that I could not take it anymore. The wake-up call for me was the fact that during the evenings, my stomach kept me racing for the bathroom. Without getting too detailed, I will just say that I could not go out with friends without worrying that I would be in the restroom most of the time. My system was completely out of synch.

I needed a better way to get my nutrition. However, when you're single, it's very tough to go home at the end of the day and prepare a full course healthy meal…. for whom? Just you? Most single people don't do it. So how does our body get the proteins and vitamins and fiber without relying on useless supplements and horse pills that really don't provide our bodies with the natural greens they need?

Juicing! Here's the easy way to get hooked on this healthy habit. Go to the grocery store and buy a small bag of carrots. You should have 3 handfuls in that bag. You may stare at those carrots and say to yourself, there is no way I want to eat those, and I certainly don't want to spend time cooking them. What's amazing here is how simple it is to simply put that handful of carrots that your body so desperately needs along with celery, wheat grass and other healthy greens and slam it into the juicer. Now you're probably thinking that this mixture is not going to taste very good. Add in 2 or 3 small apples and juice them along with the carrots, and you will be amazed at how easy, delicious, and healthy this habit becomes. What would take you 30 seconds to make and drink is something that you would probably never have the discipline to prepare and eat.

Being healthy is a mind set. I started juicing because I was tired of always being tired! I wanted more energy, and my body was crying out for it. Fad diets, crash diets and the like won't last. Juicing on a daily basis with fruits and lots of different vegetables along with regular exercise at the gym with 3 to 5 cardio workouts per week of at least 40 minutes or more will absolutely have a profound impact on your health.

Along with these changes, consider the following. Most people take better care of their fancy sports cars, houses, or jobs than they do their bodies. If you don't start treating your body as the magnificent and complex machine that it is, then you may suffer an early demise as did so many who are profiled in this book. In order to be good, you need to first feel good. If you expect to reach your goals and live the life that you truly desire, then it all starts with your body. It is just that simple!

Why Get a Heart Scan?

A CT scan is a simple, non-invasive way to detect health problems before a person shows any symptoms. Such early detection leads to better treatment outcomes and can save lives. Consider the facts, provided by heartscan.com:

Heart disease is the leading cause of death for both men and women in the United States. Current estimates show that more than 70 million Americans suffer from some form of cardiovascular disease. This "silent killer" is a slow, progressive disease that can begin early in life and go undetected for years. For 150,000 Americans annually, the first and only symptom of heart disease is a fatal heart attack. Many of those who suffer a fatal heart attack have average or unremarkable cholesterol levels, normal stress or exercise treadmill tests, and few, if any, of the major risk factors. The earlier heart disease is detected, the greater the chance it can be slowed, or stopped or possibly reversed.

Lung cancer is the leading cause of cancer deaths among men and women, as reported by the American Cancer Society. More people die of lung cancer than of colon, breast and prostate cancers combined. In 2000, approximately 164,000 new lung cancer cases were diagnosed, and there were an estimated 157,000 lung cancer deaths. If lung cancer is detected and treated early, before it has spread to lymph nodes or other organs, the 5-year relative survival rate is about 42%. However, according to the American Cancer Society, few lung cancers are detected at this early stage.

Colorectal cancers are the third most common cancers in men and women, as reported by the American Cancer Society. In 2000, an estimated 131,000 people developed colorectal cancer and an estimated 56,000 deaths occurred due to colorectal cancer. For people whose colorectal cancer is found and treated in an early stage, the 5-year relative survival rate is 90%. But, according to the American Cancer Society, only 37% of colorectal cancers are found at that early stage. Once the cancer has spread to nearby organs or lymph nodes, the 5-year survival rate drops to 65%. For those whose colorectal cancer spreads to the liver or the lungs, the 5-year relative survival rate is 8%.

My life changed one day when I was watching an episode of Oprah about heart scans. A few guests on the show were according to doctors very close to having a heart attack due to the severe blockage in their arteries, and yet these people had no idea they were ticking time bombs. They felt pretty good for the most part. This underscores how critical it is to look inside your body with these amazing new technologies to see what's really happening with your heart. Many people who appear fit, slim and in general good health could have severe problems with blocked arteries and not be aware of it. Your path towards a long and enlightened walk in life will be illuminated by your ability to look inside of your body and take control of your health.

As we have explored our finances and health and taken a close look at life saving measures that could add many years to our lives, we are now free to explore in Part 5 our path towards enlightenment. Enlightenment has been described as a concept in mysticism, philosophy, and psychology to name just a few. In Buddhism it is referred to as a state of nirvana. In defining "enlightenment," we must acknowledge the Age of Enlightenment, an eighteenth-century movement in Western philosophy that focused attention for the first time on the human body, mind, and soul. It was an age of optimism tempered by the realistic recognition of the sad state of the human condition and the need for major reforms.

My use of the word "enlightenment" has to do with transcending our daily lives and becoming very aware of our purpose for living. We are capable of being more than just humans seeking to satiate our basic needs. In the pursuit of higher living, higher forms of conscious thought, higher awareness for our walk through life, and a higher concern for others, we seek a greater enlightenment that helps us to define our purpose. The enlightened among us will ask, "will anyone know that I have lived at all?" The answer is yes, if we strive to understand the psychology of higher living and seek a path towards enlightenment. That is to say that should we seek to illuminate and discover our greater purpose, we will leave behind a footprint of a life well lived.

> *Change is the law of life, and those who look only to the past or present are certain to miss the future."*
>
> — *John F. Kennedy*

Part 5

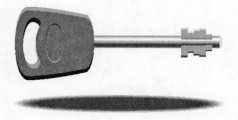

The Path to Enlightenment

THE LESSON OF STUART FRANKEL

Why are so many of us obese, unhealthy, smoking or addicted to drugs, trapped in radically dysfunctional relationships or in dead-end jobs? At the root of all of this self-abuse is the fact that we don't like ourselves very much. While some of you may be conscious of this, my question is why? Most of you have never done anything so vicious as to warrant the self-imposed sabotage that you practice. Your ability to accept yourself and learn to love yourself will set you on the path to higher living. Loving yourself does not mean reverting back to behaving as you were in your teens—self- absorbed and egocentric— rather, it's an acceptance of who you are. It's becoming comfortable with your own uniqueness and believing that you have something special to offer the world you inhabit.

Glenn Gary

My father never missed an opportunity to impart one of life's lessons, even when we were just out walking, and sometimes especially when we were out walking. One Sunday morning when I was eleven, we found ourselves ambling by Riverside Memorial Chapel on the Upper West Side of Manhattan. My father stopped right in front of the funeral home and asked me what time it was. I checked my watch and told him it was 10:25. Then he asked me what I saw going on there. "Nothing very exciting, just a crowd of people, maybe 150 in all, going into the chapel," I said.

My dad commended me for my good observation, and we continued our previous conversation about the New

York Giants. After a while, however, I realized we hadn't moved at all. We were still standing in front of the funeral chapel. Naturally, I asked why. My father didn't answer immediately, but soon he interrupted my talk of baseball with another question, as those who had entered the chapel earlier began to file out.

"What do you see now?" I shrugged.

"Well, I see all of those people who went into the chapel coming back out."

"Excellent," he said. "By the way, what time is it?"

I looked at my watch and reported it was now 10:50.

My father nodded thoughtfully. "Well, that's about right. When a person's life is over, we have a funeral to cele-brate that life, and it generally lasts about twenty minutes."

I was more than a little puzzled. "Dad, I'm only eleven. Why are we even talking about this?"

"Because I hope you will live a long and productive life, that you will be aware of your surroundings, that you will stay out of trouble, and that you will be thoughtful and cautious. And above all that you will always know in the back of your mind that someday your entire life will be summed up in twenty minutes."

> *You can't drink away your problems,*
> *For the next day you will have more.*
> *You can't get your problems high,*
> *You're already too low.*
> *You can't ignore your problems,*
> *Others around will be happy to remind you.*
> *You can't eat your problems away,*
> *You will just feel worse.*
> *You can't run away from your problems,*
> *They will still be there when you're tired.*
> *Everybody has a problem, is a problem,*

Or has to live with a problem.
Decide to turn your problems into diamonds of
opportunity, in doing so, you will reap many riches.

Glenn Gary

It's easy to forget how lucky we are to be in America. We tend to focus on negative aspects of our life in this great country such as high taxes, pollution, high gasoline prices, out of control real estate prices in states such as California, Florida and New York. We focus on who is a Democrat and who is Republican, on whether we hate or love the person in the White House. We think about our soldiers coming home in body bags, and we think about our government acquiring more and more of our personal information through our phone records, email and bank accounts. We worry that we are losing control of the border with Mexico.

I suggest that in order for us to achieve true success in our own daily lives, we must step away from our focus on the negative aspects of our own country and just for a moment look at our neighbors, Cuba and Mexico, for example; a cursory review of their economic system, lack of opportunity, poor infrastructure and corruption will give us a whole new appreciation for paying high taxes. Often we need only look at the life of another person who lacks our opportunities and we can end up feeling much better about our own. Whether you appreciate the presence of undocumented immigrants from Mexico doing work that many Americans refuse to do or strongly disagree with them being here, remember just how fortunate we are to be living in America, something that many of us forget as we get so consumed by the daily drama of our lives. Greater enlightenment in our lives requires us to step away from our own life and see a life from the eyes of someone who is much less fortunate than we are. When we do this, we allow ourselves to gain a newfound clarity on our lives as well as a compassionate focus on those around us who suffer greatly. This new found enlightenment may one day enable you to turn your considerable talents, energy and resources towards helping those around you who have much less than you. It may be to that end that a new found purpose for your life will begin to take form. Consider for a moment if you stopped and asked most people, "If you had ten million dollars, what would you do with it?" Many would say that they would help feed the hungry and bring water to the thirsty and so on. At a deep level many of us desire to help and yet we become so engulfed in our own survival that it becomes a far-off fantasy. Adopting the psychology of higher living enables you to realize that anything you set your mind to is truly possible.

ONE MAN, NO COUNTRY

People are unreasonable, illogical and self-centered.
Love them anyway.
If you do good, people will accuse you of selfish
ulterior motives.
Do good anyway.
If you are successful, you will win false friends and
true enemies.
Succeed anyway.
Honesty and frankness make you vulnerable.
Be honest and frank anyway.
The good you do today will be forgotten tomorrow.
Do good anyway.
The biggest people with the biggest ideas can be
shot down by the smallest people with the smallest
minds.
Think big anyway.
People favor underdogs but always follow top dogs.
Fight for some underdogs anyway.
What you spend years building may be destroyed
overnight.
Build anyway.
Give the world the best you've got
And you'll get kicked in the teeth.
Give the world the best you've got anyway.

Mother Theresa

A s Mother Theresa stated above, I am fighting for one of the biggest underdogs that I have ever met in my life. His name is Pablo. He is from a very poor area of Mexico. I first met Pablo more than three years ago and was impressed from day one. The day that Pablo showed up for work is one day I will never forget. While the others were laughing, messing around, and not taking the task at hand very seriously, Pablo just put his head down, and worked hard. He did not want to talk with anyone; he just got down to business. I liked him right away and wanted to help in any way that was possible. I could see that he was just a young man, working hard and trying to make his way in this world, like many of us. The following letter tells a bit of the story further.

Dear Commissioner Olson,

By the time Pablo Garcia visits your courtroom on October 18th, Pablo will have spent over 720 hours in jail surrounded by animals, not only in confinement but with his life in jeopardy. This case cries out for your attention. Eighteen years ago I too stood in front of a judge, much like Pablo Garcia did in your courtroom the other day, my life hanging in the balance. I had been driving a car and was responsible for that vehicle getting out of control and crashing. I was not drinking or doing any drugs at the time of my car accident; I was however guilty of making a split second mistake that took the life of my best childhood friend, thus ensuring that I would face a life sentence of guilt, remorse and regret.

The judge in my case took the time to read letters like the one I am writing to you from people who cared about my future. The judge recognized that putting me in jail would be a waste of my life and cause me further damage, much as it would in Pablo's situation. I am asking you to take a few minutes to consider Pablo's case. His life depends on your desire to understand that he is not like most of the hard core rapists, felons and career criminals that you encounter on a daily basis. He is the father of two baby girls, one three and the other two years old. He is hard-working; in fact every day he does the hardest of backbreaking manual labor, construction, landscaping, painting, remodeling, trash removal and other work associated with restoring homes.

There is a larger issue at stake here, Commissioner Olson; California is mired in the political debate of illegal immigration. Consider Pablo's case for a moment. He has two children depending upon him for their survival. Do you deport him back to Mexico, thus putting a further burden on our system by having his children go unsupported, or do you free him so that he can go back to work and get married to the mother of his children so that he can have a chance at a decent life? Or, as you are doing as of this writing, hold him in jail, at a cost of over $130 a day and $40,000 a year? Why would we be holding someone like Pablo in a system that should be reserved for violent criminals? By the time that he sees you on October 18th, he will have spent almost thirty days locked up. In fairness to the court, Pablo is guilty of not checking in with his probation officer. He had been picked up and deported a few months ago, and after a few weeks in Mexico made his way back to the U.S. He did not check in because he was afraid of what would happen, which was a terrible mistake on his part. I might also point out that he made his way back simply to be here so that he could support his kids. I ask you Commissioner Olson, how many American fathers make their kids their first priority, let alone risk their lives to support them? The answer is not many. This is a noble cause that the court must recognize. I would also point out that 460 people died in 2004 trying to escape the poverty of Mexico in order to reach the vast opportunity that we have in our country.

We should feel ashamed of ourselves when we stand by and watch people like Pablo Garcia struggle so hard to live. He is a hard working, honest young man caught between two countries. Unfortunately Pablo is before you due to the fact that he missed a check in with his probation officer. You have a unique opportunity to change the way the system treats people like Pablo. Judging from my three hours in your court room I would imagine eight out of ten people that come before you are deserving of the punishment of jail. Pablo does not deserve nor should he be placed in any jail, much less the vicious zoo that is LA County Men's Jail, as profiled on CNN.

Pablo deserves a second chance, either to be deported or freed. I would hope that you wouldn't go further than adding more probation time or a fine; to lock up this young man and break his spirit is a crime in itself. He is struggling to survive; he does not enjoy the opportunities that you and I enjoy. He like you Commissioner Olson is on a journey that we call life. Because of the circumstances of the country he was unlucky enough to be born into, his journey will automatically be a much more difficult one than you and I will ever experience as U.S. citizens.

I ask you to show compassion and understand that this man is just trying to survive. Pablo barely makes enough money to feed himself and his children; how can we expect him to pay for competent and more importantly committed legal help? Perhaps I know these issues all too well. I was given a second chance in 1987 and went on to lead a productive life. In 1992 I worked for a $2 billion dollar a year, publicly traded company, ABM Industries, Inc. (NYSE). ABM was built on the backs of $8.00 an hour labor, 90% of which was and is to this day, Hispanic labor.

My mother, God rest her soul used to work at the University of La Verne, right across the street from where Pablo was stopped, handcuffed and taken to jail. At the time he was doing nothing wrong; he had just received his paycheck and was walking to his car.

What will become of Pablo's two young baby girls? Do we crush them in this process? Do we break this man's spirit by throwing him in jail say for six months for not checking in with his probation department? I had a chance to sit down with Pablo's probation officer, who said the following: "Glenn, there is nothing that we can do. Sometimes we see horrible people who are beating their wives, using guns, etc. and they are set free, while good people like Pablo get sent to jail. It's not fair, but that's what happens; it's just how the system is." As his probation officer stated, all she can do is give you a report on what he has or has not done with his time on probation; it's you, Commissioner Olson, who has the power to enable Pablo to live his life.

Pablo needs to take responsibility for not showing up for probation. I understand that was wrong of him, but he was also deported. Do we say to him, stay in Mexico, and forget about your two baby girls in America? And for god's sake, does anyone like Pablo deserve to be tortured by being in LA County Men's jail, even for just one day? Hard core criminals do, but not hard working young men like Pablo, God no. I have traveled to Mexico; it is a devastated country fraught with poverty, lack of infrastructure, and corruption. But like many countries it has great people who are just looking for a chance at a decent life.

I thank you for your time and consideration.

For many of us who are better off than others, we carry a burden. It's a burden to help your fellow man or woman when you can, to recognize that we are all on a journey in this life and some of us simply by luck are granted much greater opportunity than others. It is that opportunity that almost makes me feel guilty, even after all of the tragedies and loss that I have faced in my own life. I still can't help but empathize with others who are much less fortunate. Pablo's life story is not fully written, but wherever I am, his story of struggle will follow. Hopefully all of us can take a moment out to realize that we have many blessings in this country, consider that 460 people from Mexico died trying to come to this county in 2004. 460 lost their lives because they were seeking a better life than the one they had.

CELEBRITY WORSHIP: LIVING YOUR OWN LIFE

What footprint would you like to leave behind? Will
we know that you even lived at all? How many will
show up to pay tribute to your contribution in life?
Achieving a greater awareness of yourself and sati-
ating basic needs will free you to determine your
higher purpose. In the process you will begin to
develop your footprint – one that enriches your life
and the lives of many that you meet along the way.

Glenn Gary

We are a society obsessed with celebrity. Each night we can curl up with our favorite escape mechanism, the modern day plasma HD television. Paraded in front of you, in a nightly assault on your own good common sense, are the desperate lives of Paris Hilton, Britney Spears, Lindsey Lohan, Tom Cruise, Brad Pitt and Angelina Jolie, to name just a few. For many years I have been saddened by the senseless waste of time that people devote to watching others live extraordinary lives rather than putting that time to good use in building their own extraordinary life.

Recently I got a first hand glimpse of paparazzi and its destructive force when the Hollywood train came barging into my father's neighborhood just outside of Los Angeles for a two week stay. I don't think my father was prepared for Clint Eastwood, Brad Pitt and Angelina Jolie to come to town and start filming.

The first day seemed like no big deal for most of us. I took a quick look at Jolie and Eastwood as they were filming a scene and went back to work. By day three, however, hundreds of people including paparazzi with long telephoto lens cameras were lined up for hours on end, waiting for their chance to see the stars. I made some interesting observations along the way. Throughout the course of each day, hundreds of people stood around for up to eight hours just to get a glimpse of Pitt and Jolie.

What saddened me was that people from all age groups were spending hours and day after day uprooting their own lives in order to see someone else living their life. I was tempted to construct signs and yell on a bullhorn, "Save yourselves people; use this time to construct your own life." Too much of our culture is caught up in spending hundreds of hours and lots of money watching other people live their greatest life. Higher consciousness frees you from this wasteful and toxic adulation of people who are no different than you or me; they simply get paid to be in front of a camera.

Spend enough time in LA and you'll run into them on a regular basis. When you do, you'll soon realize that you don't have the time to stop your own life for hours on end and watch others. You will be caught up in building your own cathedrals of abundance. This is truly the path of enlightenment, one that asks you to create your life and not live through others.

DEVELOPING ADVANCED LIFE MANAGEMENT SKILLS

One of the most expensive things I have ever owned was my pride. My inability to set it aside and learn from others has already cost me one fortune in my life.

Glenn Gary

Ask yourself, do you have a job, a career, or a mission? My answer in my life is that I had many jobs in my twenties, my career was becoming defined by my late twenties and early thirties, and as I enter my late thirties, I am now on my mission as a speaker, life coach, a trainer and so on. It's all about the deeper connection with people and what I can give back to others based on my journey.

Finding your true calling in life and pursuing your passion is a key to greater happiness. Nothing is worse than just working for the sake of working. You were put on this earth with special gifts. Too often, though, life just becomes a daily grind. Being stuck in the trap of doing a job you hate is a major disservice to yourself and a disservice to the company that pays your salary. Enlightenment comes from asking yourself difficult questions so that you can pursue the reality that you desire. Many people just don't ask themselves these deeper questions.

It's critical that you examine this aspect of your life and not to be afraid to go after your true passion. Don't settle for a job that you have already or will grow to resent, so that when you look back on your life, it will be filled with regret for not pursuing your dreams. Today, it's likely that the average person will experience five different careers in his or her life, so you should explore possibilities, find your passion, and pursue it with excellence. In the process you will discover your true purpose and begin to manifest a greater enlightenment for your journey through life.

> *I find it fascinating that most people plan their vacations with better care than they plan their lives. Perhaps that is because escape is easier than change.*
>
> *- Jim Rohn*

CAREER-CHANGING ACTION STEP

One way you may help yourself to find your passion is to sit down and write your own autobiography, or be a bit bolder and write your own eulogy. As strange as that may seem, you would be amazed to find the clarity that comes from having to sit down and actually write out what someone would say when your life was finished and people had gathered to remember you.

If that seems a bit much, pick the autobiography road and visualize yourself being profiled on the A&E program *Biography*; this will give you a chance to literally write the script of your future, to plan your life and its course. Few people ever actually plan their lives.

Something you should know:

The average person changes careers five times in a lifetime, and the average American lives to be 75. In 1998, about 24% of U.S. adults, an estimated 47.2 million people were smokers. Over 20 states have laws on the books that enable companies to refuse to hire smokers. That being said, smoking kills an estimated 430,000 people each year. This represents one in five deaths in the United States.

REMOVING ALL TOXINS FROM YOUR LIFE

Choose to avoid negative people and drama in your life; you will live longer.

Glenn Gary

We are surrounded by toxic people, toxic foods, toxic waste, and toxic relationships. Removing these things from your life is a first giant step forward. You know the old saying: *"You can't soar with the eagles if you're hangin with the turkeys."* Here are five simple steps that you can do immediately to take control of your body and your life. Most of us know these things, but having someone remind you of how simple it is to make significant changes in your life can make all the difference. In the seminars and coaching that I do, I am amazed at how many people don't follow these five basic principles.

ACTION STEPS:

1) If you are in a toxic relationship that is full of ups and downs, it's taking a toll on you emotionally and physically. Over a prolonged period of time the negative emotions that have become a hallmark of your relationship will start to take a toll on you physically, much as they did in my life. A toxic relationship that is chalk full of daily drama is very hard to end, as it usually has taken you several months to become entrenched in it. We seem to suspend our good judgment and become "addicted" to toxic people in a narcissistic way. It is only when we become sick and tired of being sick and tired that we break free. The amazing part of this trans-

formation is you'll look back a few months or even years later and wonder why this toxic person was able to have such a hold on you. The final answer will always be because you gave that person the power, through your need for their attention and/or your own low self-esteem. It is important to realize that some people survive off of creating drama, and if you want to live a healthy life you need to run as fast from them as possible. Regardless of how beautiful these people may be physically, they are poisoning your life.

2) Resolve to spend the $150 on a top of the line juicer and start feeding your body the carrots, squash, apples, celery and other vegetables that your body requires. If you make sure that you put apples into the juicer each time, you'll be assured of having a great tasting juice drink that will change your body chemistry, which ultimately changes your mind, your thinking and your overall effectiveness in the game of life.

3) As an eleven year veteran of Starbucks, I have assaulted my body on a daily basis with caffeine. Over the past five years I have made a habit of cleansing my body with lots of water. You can spend hundreds of dollars purchasing detox kits from health food stores and go to health spas for the painful and dare I say emotionally charged experience of getting a colonic (colon hydrotherapy), or you can simply help your body remove toxins and help your mind fight off depression by simply flushing your system with plenty of water every day. Toxic foods zap us of the vital energy that our body was designed for and desperately needs in order to deal with the stress of life.

4) Resolve to form a supportive group of self-actualized friends. End your relationships with envious, jealous or

destructive "friends." Remember that the right friends lift us, the wrong ones hurt us. Sometimes even a "family member" can be toxic; resolve to stay away from people who bring you down, even if they're your family. I chose to stay away from my father for many years due to the destructive forces that were a hallmark of our relationship. This helped to free my mind so that I could focus on building a better life, rather than what many people spend their time on, which is stirring up and being embroiled in drama.

5) Incorporating yoga into your life is one of the best detoxifying exercises you can practice. Because one of the foundations of yoga is breathing, and one of the ways to detoxify yourself is to simply breathe, yoga can give you the ability to make the most out of every breath you take. The poses, or Asanas, practiced in yoga also aid in detoxification. Freeing the body of restrictions, these Asanas stretch muscles and limbs, loosening them and letting the muscles and limbs become more relaxed and nimble, freeing the toxins that muscle knots may harbor. These Asanas aid in circulation, and the circulation of blood is greatly enhanced through flexibility. These poses make you flow better physically and mentally. When your body fluids flow correctly, the body rids itself of toxins much more easily. Yoga also circulates positive thinking, which removes toxins from the body in more ways than one. A person bent on negative thinking will not only perpetuate thoughts laden in toxicity, but they are also more likely to engage in an overall unhealthy lifestyle, a lifestyle that invites impurities rather than fights them.

GETTING ORGANIZED

*We know that the right friends lift us, the wrong
ones hurt us. The question to ask yourself is what
type of friend are you to others?*

Glenn Gary

My struggle with clutter began after my mother died when I had to put her belongings in storage. My mother's death took a heavy toll on my life at the time, and I was soon moving from place to place. Forget about being a professional speaker—I should have owned a moving and storage truck, I moved around so much. For many years in my early to late twenties, I rented a large storage shed. Still, the amount of my personal stuff along with the weight of all of my mothers belongings were dragging me down.

Far too many people can't even walk around in their own garage because it's so full of junk. After years of this type of situation, I resolved to free my life of clutter. No more closets full of junk. No more garages or storage sheds or messy files. It took a period of a few years devoted to letting go of "stuff" to move past the emotional baggage that had filled my head.

You will feel an incredible sense of renewed energy when you have finally decided to free your life of messy desks, overstuffed file cabinets and cluttered rooms. Keep in mind that this clutter represents chaos, and if we are to reach the true potential that is in all of us, we must first free our lives from clutter. What brought me to this point was buying a shiny new sports car that I treasured so much that I couldn't imagine the thought of having it sit outside overnight. It took a whole weekend, but I finally made that last liberating move to resolve to throw out everything that was in my garage so that I could park my new car in it.

I have coached many people who have literally become hostage to this chaos, the junk that we choose to hang onto in our lives. We have come into this world with nothing, no-thing, and we will leave with nothing. To hold onto closets and garages full of "stuff" is to simply choose to not live to our greatest potential. In essence we choose to walk around with rooms of baggage, physical and emotional, instead of doing the heavy lifting of removal.

When you DECIDE to finally do this, you will find an amazing level of clarity! I guarantee it.

DEFINE YOURSELF BY CREATING YOUR PURPOSE

Who are you? Are you what others say you are?
Are you the person that you want to be?
Are you living your life in someone else's shadow?
Or do you stand up, take control of your life, and
live it to the fullest potential?
Are you defined by what your partner is or does?
Are you the CEO of your own life or the secretary
of some one else's?
Are you lost in the chase of another's affection?
Or are you busy in your own chase and pursuit of
your own dreams?
Do you see each day as you see a dollar?
We must decide how we're going to spend each
dollar.
Do you see each day as the treasure that it is?
Or do you see each day like any other, carelessly
letting it waste away?

Glenn Gary

Many things define my life. I have gained strength from so many areas. On two occasions I've jumped from airplanes at over 12,000 feet. Each time I have come away feeling empowered. I've been homeless with no place to go and no one to turn to; I've had people taken from me, and I've been responsible for the loss of another's life. What is important is that each tragedy or setback in my life has made me stronger. Each time I lose at something I come away feeling as if I have gained new wisdom. Each failure only helps to make me stronger. I feel now as though I can handle any setback in my life, no matter how tragic. It might be that feeling comes from already having lost so much, but nonetheless I feel only encouraged by all of my disappointments. They have strengthened my resolve to succeed.

We should think of our setbacks as badges of honor. When soldiers prepare for battle, face fears, enter the battle, and emerge victorious, they are stronger for having gone through it. They witness horrible human suffering, which causes them to draw upon an inner strength they might not have known they had.

Life is like a battle, even a full-out war at times. To survive, and also thrive, we must reach deep down to find that inner strength. Many people choose to compound their problems with more problems, or to heap more misery on top of their existing misery. This only leads to self-destruction. I would submit that people should take control of their setbacks, search for the good things in life, and weather the storm. If you do this, you will be victorious in the end. Walk tall and wear your setbacks as badges of honor. It's always your choice.

One of our greatest presidents, Abraham Lincoln, once stated: *"In the end, it's not the years in your life that count. It's the life in your years."* In my opinion, once we have satiated our basic needs, we can move towards putting our thoughts, time and energy into finding our true purpose in life. I would have you ask your self this very challenging question, "What am I doing here in this life, and why do I do what I do?" Why is finding your purpose so important? The answer is simple, but finding your purpose may require some heavy lifting. Finding your purpose in life will allow you to stop getting up in the morning and going to a job that you hate or dislike just so that you can pay the bills. It will show you the difference between doing something just for the money or doing something during your time here on this earth that you feel inspired to do, that you're passionate about. When you wake up in the morning, you will have the feeling that you are being true to yourself, that what you do is making a difference in your life and in other people's lives, and that you have reached deep down inside and are doing something with a skill or a talent that you have developed.

I grew up in a family of teachers. My father taught junior high woodshop and math for almost 20 years. When I look back, I think he hated almost every day of it, or at least it seemed like he hated it. He was constantly complaining about the system, the district and their lack of funding for programs and so on. The interesting dichotomy is that he was a great teacher.

When school let out, he turned his considerable talents at carpentry to doing construction jobs for friends. In fact he could build an entire house with his hands if he wanted. Yet even this seemed to contribute to his unhappiness. I'll never forget a room addition and bathroom remodel he did many years ago for a colleague. It turned into the job from hell, and he spent a lot of time screaming and yelling, angry at himself for bidding it too low, not really liking the hard work. In short, he was constantly miserable. As he fades into the twilight of his time here, I can look back over the landscape of his life and honestly tell you that he hated most everything that he did. He never took the time to ask himself what he really wanted to do and then summon the courage to go do it.

The flip side of that dark coin is my mother, who, when she died, was getting her teaching credential and absolutely loved working with kids. While she was in school she also worked full time at an infant center, and though the work was hard, it brought so much joy to her.

I would suggest to you that finding your true purpose in life is going to be one of the most important issues that you will ever address in life. If you find your purpose and go to work on it, you will feel a burning desire and passion for life. If you don't find your purpose, like my father you will trudge through each heavy day feeling constantly frustrated. True enlightenment is when we seek greater awareness for everything that is in our life; we question whether it is good for us. Your purpose in life can change. You may not always have the same purpose. How do you know if your purpose changes? You know when what you love to do changes. To me it is that simple. Or maybe you are sitting in a cubicle working for a company and wondering, why am I here? Maybe you have the corner office and you're a senior executive but you are also asking yourself that same question. Maybe you have been doing the same thing just with a few different employers over that time period, but you know that it's not something that you really love to do. Maybe you're like many people I have encountered who just fell into their careers. They have progressed, but there is still that nagging lingering feeling that they are not doing what they think they are capable of.

In *The 100th Human*, author Chris Fenwick once said of finding your purpose:

"The average Westerner, some would label civilized (I would not choose that word), is caught in a life of mediocrity and unhappiness. The magic has been lost on most. We are sucked into the spell of consumerism, to be left with many things in our garage but nothing in our hearts. We live frustrated, desperate lives of hopelessness, which are only occasionally sprinkled with moments of hope and clarity. The most we look forward to is the next thing we can add to our already bulging pile of stuff. We somehow go to jobs we don't choose, day in day out, wondering if there isn't something more to life. We skimp and scrape to get by, never thinking about the next person. It does not often cross our

minds that giving away our time, energy and love to another, gives us more happiness and hope in our own lives. We live in fear – fear of dying, fear of living, fear of losing our stuff, fear of our neighbors, fear of the environment, fear of change, and fear of ourselves, really."

I can honestly say that I have not let fear of change prevent me from rethinking my career. I look back as I approach 40 and the midway point of my life, and I think about all the different things that I have done over the past 18 or 19 years of my working life. For several years in my twenties I was in sales. I finally came to a point in my late twenties where I did not want to seek financial security as a worker for someone else's company. Instead I wanted to be my own boss, and at the same time I wanted to do something that I have never done before, so I did a 180 in my life and went into investment banking. I studied for my Series 7 securities license, worked with other people that had a lot of experience in IPO's, and in short, did everything I could to learn as much as I could and as fast as I could.

However, many things in our economy move in cycles; for six years we saw a very hot housing market that allowed investors, mortgage brokers, real estate professionals and many other people make lots of money from the housing sector. But now companies like Countrywide and the recently failed Indy Mac Bank and many others are laying off thousands of workers and consumers are seeing lots of equity roll off the table, something we also saw with the stock market and the dot coms. The point is, there are cycles to our economy, and many people have moved with those cycles. I myself have moved into industries because the opportunity was indeed very good, but chasing cycles and pursuing opportunity because a housing market heats up or the stock market is hot and you think you can make a million as a day trader is not necessarily finding your purpose.

Some people like my father can say, "Hey I was a teacher and that's what I did for 20 years." However, entrepreneurs tend to evolve into more than one thing; in fact there is a study out that suggests the average person in the United States will have between 5 and 7 careers in their lifetime, which is an amazing change from how things were just 30 years ago. In the 50's and 60's it was typical to grow up, go to school, get a good job and stay at the same company and retire after 30 or 40 years. Now, more than likely you will have to (or currently need to) reinvent yourself.

Finding your purpose might be easier than you think, since your purpose might be the same as something you dream about doing. You may be a teacher, but having kids and raising a family is calling you. You could be dreaming about opening a restaurant but have been too afraid to take out the equity from your home and take the risk. Maybe you're like my friend who always dreamed of being a wine maker, so he finally one day decided to purchase two acres of property in Mexico to start a vineyard. Since he lives in San Diego, he can afford to drive the hour and a half it takes to get to his vineyard, and now he has crushed his first harvest of grapes and within the year will finally be bottling his own private label wine, this after taking classes in wine making and over a two year period building a new house on the land and so on. Maybe you have always wanted to open up your own women's clothing boutique or a daycare for kids or an animal shelter, but you have just been too afraid.

You see, there is no right answer; no one should ever define for you what your purpose is. Only you can find it deep within you. I like the way my good friend Steve went after finding his purpose. During the 50's, he was a Hollywood actor who starred in films along with Frank Sinatra, Dean Martin and many others. Though he was under contract with MGM, his true passion was dancing, and for many years he operated a very successful dance studio and did very well for himself. He put on lots of productions and taught many famous people how to dance, in essence following his calling. As he got into his late 40's, he discovered his passion for wine and food and turned his studio into a very profitable and unique Italian restaurant. It was a financial risk at the time in the mid-seventies, but as I sat next to him during his final hour of life at the age of 76, I felt honored to be there with someone who had indeed lived a full life with true purpose.

Sometimes finding your purpose is about doing something that may not involve money. People tend to follow money as the guiding force to making career decisions, but your purpose does not always have to be attached to a dollar. We all see the world differently. For instance, I had a nagging feeling of wanting to connect with others and share my experiences in the hopes that they could help people. But it goes deeper than a feeling. You can identify the feeling, but I am asking you to go deeper and ask yourself what that feeling would actually look like if it were manifested in your day to day life.

For me it was that I wanted to speak in front of hundreds of people, and I felt that if I did not write books, get up and speak, then I was somehow not utilizing all that I was and am capable of. You must ask these questions of yourself: what have you not done that you think you're capable of doing? What talent lies inside of you that you are not using? What skill sets have you developed but don't exploit? What hobby or passion do you have that you have always wanted to turn into a business?

When you discover your purpose and go after it, you will then feel that your life has the meaning that you have always desired. I recently played a tennis match with a doctor who worked as a emergency room physician. Prior to med school he was a teacher. I asked him if he liked what he did, and how he could handle the blood and gore of seeing people come into the emergency room with gunshots or head wounds from car accidents. He said, "Glenn, this is my purpose; it was something I always wanted to do, and I kept putting it off until I finally made the decision. Saving lives was more rewarding to me than trying to help a kid learn to read when that kid did not want to be in my class in the first place. I felt I needed and wanted to be saving lives in that emergency room." He is on purpose and he is doing something that makes a difference in his life. It may not be what I could do or you could do, but to him it matters, and that's the whole point. Finding and pursuing your purpose is about connecting with what you really want to do, and what you think you could do to contribute to the world. Whether that's opening a mortuary and helping people make final arrangements, or buying a farm, or opening a flower shop, it does not matter. However, many people are so bogged down with just trying to make a living that they don't think about their purpose, despite the fact that they don't like what they do. When we meet people who are living on-purpose, we revere them, call them heroes and envy their lives. We each have our own gifts to bring.

> *Life isn't about finding yourself. Life is about creating yourself.*
>
> —*George Bernard Shaw*

DEVELOPING YOUR WORLD VIEW

> *The sick person, with a proclivity to feel his life has no meaning, can still become pregnant with a future that holds unlimited opportunities to help his fellow man. In the process, he transcends his existential angst and adopts a cause that is greater than his own. Should you choose to engage in higher living, you will surrender your ego and adopt this consciousness. It is one that will illuminate the suffering of those who may be in a far off land, forgotten by the many, but remembered by the enlightened who, in turn, choose to take action.*
>
> Glenn Gary

We have two choices. We can be local citizens that tend to our own gardens, choosing to go to work each day, come home, feed our own kids, and live our own lives on a very local, community basis. Or we can decide that we are truly citizens of the world, here on this planet to make a huge and lasting impact. That is, we can truly save lives. I often ask myself how I want to look back on my life when I am sixty, seventy or eighty years old. Did I want to live my life just caught up in worrying about how I was going to pay my bills, move my career forward, manage my FICO score, my blood pressure and just worry about myself? Or can I transcend my own situation, regardless of how wealthy and healthy I am or am not and truly develop a world view. I am reminded by one of history's great thinkers, James Allen who simply stated: "As a man thinketh in his heart, so is he." I ask you, what is in your heart, what do you think about when it comes to helping others? For me it became clear that I chose to always be stuck just focusing on my own problems, deciding that there was no room for anyone else's problems. As I looked deeper into my own thinking, I discovered the chasm that remains between truth and reality. The greatest truth is that which the individual chooses to act upon. Of course these actions help to shape our reality. I noticed a massive change and reduction in my own anxiety levels and fear of how I would survive, pay the bills etc. These anxieties and fears seemed to almost completely go away when I finally decided to acknowledge and learn about the suffering of others. I am not referring to the type of suffering of a Joe six-pack who just lost his job at the warehouse. I am referring to over one billion people on this planet that don't even have access to clean drinking water. The more I investigated this, the more I realized that I don't have problems in my life. I have challenges, but I don't have problems. Not having clean drinking water, understanding that 9 million children a year die from malnutrition and disease in this world, that's a problem. Being 30 or 60 days late on your mortgage is just a challenge, one that you will eventually solve.

For many years I chose to not get involved because I did not feel that one person could make any type of impact. I also did not like how I could not determine where or how much of each dollar would actually go towards the intended cause. I also wanted to actually be directly involved as opposed to just feeling guilty watching a news report on Hurricane Katrina victims, for example, and trudging over to the desk and scratching the obligatory check so as to sooth my guilt. We channel surf late at night to unwind and the eventual picture of hungry children pops on the TV and screams into our consciousness. Disturbed we quickly change the channel so as to emancipate ourselves from the rush of guilt that we feel as we sit in bed, carton of Hagen Doz in one hand and our finger on the remote in the other.

Let me say this was me for many years. However, I have witnessed my own self-induced suffering reduce very dramatically the more I stopped turning away from the suffering of others. In essence it becomes an awakening that engulfs your soul and brings a new found meaning to your existence. This change marks a distinctive and profound change in your life. This brings us to a crisis that engulfs many of us in modern society today. To shine a brighter light, let's go back some fifty years and bathe in the philosophy of one of the 20th century's greatest theologians. Paul Tilich, in his seminal book, *The Courage to Be*, in my view is very cogent in helping us to examine the plight of modern man. He once stated that: "*There is something astonishing in the American courage for an observer who comes from Europe. A person may have experienced a tragedy, a destructive fate, the breakdown of convictions, even guilt and momentary despair: he feels neither destroyed nor meaningless nor condemned nor without hope. When the Roman Stoic experienced the same catastrophe he took them with courage of resignation. The typical American, after he has lost the foundations of his existence, works for new foundations. This is true of the individual and it is true of the nation as a whole.*"

That pretty much describes my mindset and serves as the catalyst for driving home the following point. Regardless of how much our homes have dropped in value or whether gas is $4.00 per gallon or $7.00 as some predict it may be in the coming years, we can choose to step away. Perhaps we can let go of the endemic ambivalence that chokes us and consumes our thoughts. In its place we immediately set aside self-centered, egocentric desires to just worry about our own problems and we get involved in the plight of a people who don't even know what the hell a FICO score is, what it means to even drive a car, much less own one and couldn't tell you the difference between a cell phone or the remote control on your TV.

I for one have grown weary and tired of just thinking about myself all the time. It's great when your 17, but the older I get, the more bored I have become with just thinking about Glenn. I submit to you that if you think of it in this type of context, you may liberate yourself from this lower consciousness. In so doing, you will find it to be quite a defining moment in your life. ·

Are You Extrinsically Motivated?

This is the desire to perform an act, a behavior based upon the potential external rewards that may be received. Often people who operate from this type of thinking do so for the rewards such as money or grades. These rewards provide satisfaction and pleasure that the task may not provide.

Are You Intrinsically Motivated?

This is the motivation or desire to do something based on the enjoyment of the behavior and not on what you'll get from it. This comes from inside the individual rather than from external or outside rewards such as money or grades. This type of person does not work on a task because there is a reward, prize, payment or grade involved.

Manifesting the Life That You Desire

Charlie Rose, one of our most compelling voices of intelligent discourse that permeates the airwaves today, stated it best when he said: "Some people look at their lives and say this is what I was born to do. Somehow we must find the right convergence of passion, skill and temperament in order to have a sense of pride and accomplishment over one's lifetime."

RYAN'S WELL

Our quest for personal development is much like
being a detective, weeding through the mine field
until we have discovered or uncovered the meaning
in our lives.

Glenn Gary

SIX-YEAR-OLD Ryan Hreljac sat in shock as he listened to his first grade teacher, Nancy Prest, at Holy Cross Catholic School in Kemptville, Ont. Launching a school-wide campaign, she spoke that day of the sad plight of children living in impoverished, disease-stricken Africa, where there was little access to medicine, food or clean water. Ryan, a sensitive child with blond hair and blue eyes, winced when he heard that hundreds of thousands of African children die each year just from drinking contaminated water.

It was January 1998, and Holy Cross was raising money for African relief. "Every penny helps," Prest told her class. She explained that a single penny would buy a pencil; 25 cents, 175 vitamins; 60 cents, a two-month supply of medicine for one child; "and $70 pays for a well."

When Ryan's mother, Susan, 40, a consultant at the Ontario Ministry of Citizenship, Culture and Recreation, and Mark, his police-officer father, got home later that day, Ryan rushed past his baby-sitter to greet them. "Mom, Dad, I need $70 for a well in Africa!" he said excitedly.

And so began the journey for Ryan that would last several more years as he raised money for clean water in Africa. As it turned out, the seventy dollars needed to drill a well was really more like two thousand dollars. But after several years, Ryan, with the help of friends, family and the local community, would end up raising an astonishing $1 million dollars. As a little boy, Ryan and his family made the trek to Africa and several other countries.

His first project was a well for Angolo Primary, a school that was in an area suffering from 13 years of rebel activity, several years of drought and the scourge of AIDS. The closest water source was a swamp five kilometres away. Many of the children had large, extended bellies from infestations of intestinal worms. At any given time, nearly a quarter of the students had diarrhea. Typhoid and other deadly water-borne diseases were also common. With no doctors in the area of 31,850 people, one in five children died before age five.

Since Angolo Primary School and the community began using Ryan's well for their cooking and drinking water, the rates of diarrhea infections and water-borne disease have dropped. Ryan's fund-raising continues to this day, and as of this writing, he isn't even in college yet. At last count he has helped raise over $60,000 for new drilling and well-construction equipment in Uganda. With CIDA's contributions, the funds have built more than 30 wells. And in the seven years since, this ordinary, yet extraordinary Canadian schoolboy has raised the many hundreds of thousands of dollars needed to fund 170 water and sanitation projects in 9 countries, including Zimbabwe, Ethiopia, Kenya, Uganda, Tanzania, Zambia, Nigeria, Malawi, Ghana, Burkina Faso India, Guyana, and Guatemala.

So take heart: there is much you can do to make this world a better place. Simply begin by doing the best you can, and who knows where that might lead. Ryan clearly demonstrates that you don't need to be a Bono, or an Oprah. If a little boy from Canada can raise his awareness, develop a higher consciousness at the meager age of just twelve and convince his mother and father to fly him and his family to Africa and build wells, thus radically changing lives in the process, then you and I can certainly transcend our daily lives and make extraordinary contributions to this world. We don't have to be wealthy in order to do it. Pursing higher living and developing a greater awareness of your walk in life will enable you to contribute much like Ryan has. In the process, you will transcend your existence, constructing something that will hold much greater meaning.

ACCEPTANCE OF OTHER PEOPLE'S SUCCESS: ARE YOU READY?

Seeking greater awareness of why you do what you do will unlock all the possibilities that are available to you. Most people choose to not seek greater understanding, thus they fall short of their fullest potential.

Glenn Gary

For many of us, (including myself up until a certain point in my own life) it can be difficult to avoid feeling envious of people in our lives who have achieved significant levels of success. I believe that many people feel this way but would never think of admitting this to themselves at a conscious level. Envy is pervasive in our society, yet it is a very limiting and debilitating feeling to hold onto.

In my view, envy evolves from the feelings of massive inadequacy that arise when we have failed to achieve our goals. For men, these feelings are triggered for example when the "other guy" pulls up in a Porsche or high end Mercedes. It can happen when we visit another person's mansion and compare it to our own modest abode. However, these desires for material possessions weaken our state of being. If we are to live life at higher levels of consciousness, we come to learn that a fancy car or big home should not and certainly does not define us. Rather these are just objects meant to satiate our egos.

As you begin to search inside yourself and identify what your true purpose is and set out to explore and develop that purpose, you will begin to be freed from thoughts of envy. You will realize that while others around you may have carved out their niche and beaten you to it, your time is coming.

This realization was a significant development for me. Some time ago I had a conversation with a friend who declared: "Glenn, I met with my accountant today and he declared that I am a millionaire, given all of the assets that I own." Ten years earlier, I would have been feeling quite envious, but due to my confidence about my own purpose in life, I felt truly happy for him and congratulated him on his success. A few years back I became friends with a professional major league baseball player, one whose contract paid him over seventy million dollars. On our frequent shopping trips to Rodeo Drive in Beverly Hills, I would see him spend ten grand on a watch, yet I did not flinch with envy. Why should I if I truly have a higher consciousness?

When you achieve self-actualization, you begin to accept other people and their own greatness on their own terms. You simultaneously stop focusing on everyone around you and focus instead on your own genius. Crossing this hurdle in my life and coming to terms with other people's significant accomplishments and success, even if I was not there yet myself, gave me an awesome sense of freedom. It takes quite a bit of negative energy to be consumed with jealousy and envy. I realized that by letting go of these thoughts and searching inward to define my own unique abilities, I could more easily become fully self-actualized. In essence, it was part of my ability to achieve my own full potential.

9 PRINCIPLES OF SUCCESS

A life lived with limited understanding will only yield you limited gains. Ask yourself "am I applying critical thinking to all facets of my life?" If the answer is no, ask yourself why not?

Glenn Gary

The following nine principles for success have quite literally taken me many years to collect and fully adopt in my own life. They have come from my many years of personal self-discovery and life experiences as well as those of other people, all of which I have passed on in my seminars.

These nine principles are presented with the hope that once adopted, they will give you a deeper and richer experience in your walk through life. They are outlined so that you can use them to create the kind of life that you really want. Most of us want a sense of purpose, but we get bogged down in being what others want us to be or in being defined by our material achievements.

It's critical that we reach a point where we can confidently say "I am a successful human being living the life that I always wanted." I hope that these principles will guide your life, but they only work if you allow them to work. They have nothing to do with the material world; they have to do with looking inside yourself. Some of this wisdom was shared with me, and some has come from the many setbacks that I have learned to turn into success. It is with great joy that I pass them along to you. I feel that it is a necessity in life to pass along good habits and great wisdom while breaking the cycle of broken families and poisoned minds.

People who have been able to achieve any meaningful level of success credit this in large part to their overwhelming burning desire to accomplish that success. When told their goals were too lofty, these people used the skepticism and doubt of others to push themselves even harder. It's that burning desire that let them know they would not be at peace or feel any sense of fulfillment unless their goals were met.

Living your life in a way that is independent of what others feel you should be doing with your life is a vital first step towards self-actualization. Consult yourself as to what is right for you, regardless of what others may think.

The nine principles:

OPEN YOUR MIND TO LEARNING NEW WAYS OF RESPONDING TO OTHERS, AND DETACH YOUR MIND FROM YOUR EGO

Having an open and detached mind is vital for our own self-preservation. Most people spend their lives looking for reasons to be offended by the reactions from those around us. I remember when I first heard this idea from a seminar that I was watching, and the very next day the following happened to me. I was picking my mail up from my postal box. I had been a long term customer and happened to be dressed in a suit that day, so of course I looked like a decent, bill paying human being. The clerk brought my mail out and stated "that will be $20.00 please for the past due on your monthly rental." I noticed that she set the mail behind her rather than handing it to me, and I felt pretty angry by the notion that she did not have the respect to trust that I would not grab my mail and bolt from the store like a common criminal. I was tempted to say something to her right in front of everyone. However, although I was irritated by her lack of consideration, I chose to let it go. It wasn't worth embarrassing her or myself by causing a scene.

In a similar situation, my father did not show such restraint. One day he and I decided to get some ice cream at Baskin Robbins. Mind you I was in my thirties at this point, not a child along for the ride. I had gotten my ice cream and was heading back to the car when I heard this wild screaming from the store. I look back in utter embarrassment to see my father screaming and ranting at some teenage clerk who probably did not give him the respectful tone that he needed in order to complete his ice cream purchase. He blew out of the store with a disgusted look as though he had just been assaulted.

The point is that even when you are offended, you can choose to take a calm approach rather than one that will result in you looking like some crazed madman. How pleasant it would be for you and everyone around you if, when you feel offended, you simply and quietly pull someone aside and explain how you feel without getting hysterical.

Detachment means having an open mind that is open to everything and attached nowhere. That does not mean that we don't love and commit to a person or a group of family members, but it does mean that we are not emotionally destroyed when they do not act or behave the way we expect. Self-preservation depends on achieving this kind of emotional independence.

This type of attachment is a hard habit to break. However, remember that progress in your life is impossible if you always do things the way you have done things. It's like that old saying: the definition of insanity is expecting a different outcome when you engage in the same behavior over and over again.

YOU CAN'T GIVE OF YOURSELF THAT WHICH IS NOT INSIDE OF YOU

You can't give away what you don't have. People who don't have love inside themselves, for example, cannot give it away. Many of us have heard this time and time again. If you have anger and contempt inside yourself, then you will give that away. For example, if we are at a point in our lives where we feel self-defeated, it's very hard to be loving towards others. This is because we are so consumed by our own feelings of failure.

A life that is filled with "an ocean of abundance" is only possible when we change our way of dealing with others. If your message to the world is "give me, give me," you will always be in a state of feeling neglected. If you change your message to "how may I serve you," it's amazing how your world and the people in it will respond. In my many years of business I have seen too many people only out for that almighty dollar, a goal by the way that is very clear to others. People can sense that you don't care. Instead think about Kennedy's often quoted command: "Ask not what your country will do for you, but what you can do for your country." Like any great truth, it stands the test of time and generations.

HANGING ONTO JUSTIFIED RESENTMENTS ONLY WEAKENS YOU

This was for me and many people very difficult to embrace. Many of you carry around resentment about people, for example, who owe you money, people who walked out on you, people who have abused you, people who fired you, and much of this resentment is justified. Those resentments, though, will always end up harming you and filling you with despair and anger.

I can state for certain that this is true. I have heard this for many years, and I have lived it. In my early and mid twenties I experienced this destructive resentment. But the sooner you let go of your focus on these injustices and turn your incredible talents and energy towards re-drafting your reality, your new energy will carry you to greater achievements. Success takes energy, so re-direct the negative energy of resentment towards new success. For more than fifteen years I held serious resentment towards my own father for his many failures to provide for us. Once I was able to let that go and realize that it was no longer necessary, I was freed from that prison of thought. My relationship with him works now because I place no expectations on him.

When we free ourselves from expecting things from our parents, we transcend the resentment that goes along with these expectations and can then engage in a positive relationship that is free of the burden of dependence, which only sets us up for massive disappointment.

You can use these same techniques in your career. If you unite people with you instead of against you in the corporate world, you will travel up that ladder much more quickly. Look at your corporate job much like a politician who is trying to build a consensus. Think of it as having friends gathered around you at the bottom of the ladder, pushing you up. After you take a couple of steps up, all your friends gather to push you even higher. Your whole body is being pushed up the ladder because you have united people with you instead of what most people do, which is to alienate people through confrontations, bad mouthing, gossip, etc. If you treated everyone with this contempt you would not win an election, and you certainly won't get very far in your career either.

DON'T DIE WITH YOUR MUSIC STILL INSIDE YOU; INSTEAD FIND THE COURAGE TO GO AFTER YOUR TRUE CALLING

All of us have our own music playing, and all of us have an incredible and heroic mission. As I sit in Starbucks working on my book and listening to obnoxious teenagers create a ruckus, I know that it may take a while for some, but it's clear to me that we all show up here in this life with a purpose. Too many of us are afraid to listen to that music and march to it.

EMBRACE PEACEFUL MOMENTS

Get quiet, get peaceful. We live such fast paced lives; we hit the freeways driving 80 mph in life's fast lane. We are constantly listening to radios, televisions, loud music and other people's voices, opinions, needs, wants etc. In the world of Zen, they say it's the space between the bar that holds the tiger, and it's the silence between the notes that makes the music. When you sit in your own backyard or in a park somewhere and allow yourself to experience silence, you will begin to feel more connected.

GIVE UP YOUR PERSONAL STRUGGLE. DON'T FORGET IT, BUT STOP CARRYING THE HEAVY BAG THAT HAS BEEN YOUR HISTORY

All of us carry large and heavy garbage bags filled with our past, with all the things and people that have harmed us, and we willingly carry this bag. Many hold onto this bag as if it were money or precious drinking water and refuse to let go of it. We bond ourselves to these wounds of our past and for many of us, including my own father, our identity comes from this garbage bag full of wrongs.

Moving yourself into the now, into this very moment, and letting go of the past is vital. Here is how to do this: Handle your past like you would handle a broken antique that you have always loved. Embrace it, understand it, and accept it. Say to yourself "I had to go through these things in order to become the person that I am today, and I don't need to carry around the evidence all the time." My father needed his evidence; he would constantly invite you to look inside his garbage bag, desperate for you to see it and feel it and to share in his misery. Finally, you simply throw it away, giving up your attachment to your past. Strive to stop obsessing over it, and instead, focus your new energy towards solutions. Few things in life waste more time than this.

REINVENT YOUR THINKING

Bathe your intellect each night and each week with a new book. This will have a profound impact on your thinking and will forever leave an imprint on your life as you adopt the wisdoms from the many great authors, philosophers and leaders of the world. Make your mind a repository for new thinking. Invite wisdom in and in the process your life will expand to the limitless possibilities that await you. Engaging and exposing my intellect in a vigorous absorption of books has completely changed the way I look at the world, helping to shape and give me a larger world view along with how I view my own life. Always remember that leaders are readers.

DEVELOP A ZERO TOLERANCE FOR NEGATIVE INFORMATION

Completely disengage and develop a zero tolerance for negative sources of information. On a daily basis, your consciousness is assaulted with murder, mayhem and human destruction beamed to you via satellite. Over many years, your conscious and sub-conscious mind has been bombarded with how negative life can be. This is a distorted fallacy, but we hardly recognize how wonderful and beautiful life is by tuning in to negative sources that only serve to dumb us down and leave us feeling depressed. For example, several years ago I made a conscious effort to start watching PBS, which in my view is one of the last bastion's of intelligent, thought-provoking and utterly stimulating Television that exists in the stratosphere today. Knowhere will you find such intelligent discourse on our modern life than you will by watching programs such as Nova, Charlie Rose, Tavis Smiley, and the many wonderful PBS specials that bring you some of this world's finest speakers, critical thinkers and information. Tune into NPR, National Public Radio and start finding new sources to grow your mind.

REPROGRAM YOUR MIND; REWRITE YOUR CONTRACT WITH REALITY

Resolve problems in your life by changing your mind. As a great speaker once said, "It is your mind where they live, it is your mind that created them and it is there where you experience all illusions." Simply resolve to rewrite your agreement with your reality. I have found it amazing that Hollywood movie studios and directors will spend millions of dollars and hundreds of hours crafting scripts about people's lives and then hand these scripts over to other humans who will now spend weeks and months of their lives pretending to be someone else, all so one main human, the director, the person living his or her life, can now order others to create the director's artistic vision.

Yet we can't seem to sit down and write our own script of how we want our lives to go. We can write a business plan or college papers, but can't seem to write the script of our lives. That makes little sense to me.

One of the most difficult things to do in the world is to admit that you are wrong. Admit that in some areas of your life, you have been making choices that are not working, and decide to no longer make those choices. As you might expect, the results in your life will also start to change.

Greater awareness of yourself on your path towards enlightenment begins to take shape when you avoid all thoughts that weaken you. These can be thoughts of anger and disappointment, thoughts that I have experienced quite a bit. We know that to hold onto anger, fear, anxiety, worry and other negative emotions takes quite a bit of our precious energy; the key is to shift those thoughts to more productive thoughts, hopefully to love and kindness.

> *"You can't solve a problem with the same mind that created it."*
>
> *Albert Einstein*

GREATER ENLIGHTENMENT THROUGH LIVING THE TAO

If you are tired of our warped society that tracks every move Britney Spears and Paris Hilton make and actually puts a value on who these so-called celebrities are dating, then I think you will find digesting the principles of the Tao to be quite a refreshing break. In a world that views news as accounts of murder, mayhem, terrorism and the local person found dead in a trash can behind some abandoned building, the effects of the Tao on our modern society and into your consciousness is long over due.

Glenn Gary

The Tao Te Ching has in just a short period of time resonated with me at a deep level and made a profound impact on my life. The Tao has changed how I view the world; it has shown me how our egos dominate our actions, our thoughts, and our responses to others, how the urge to gain more material wealth can be less effective than just simply living in the now and being content with where you are today and appreciating your existence.

Often I will sit and read the Tao for an hour or so, and I find these versus so uplifting and thought provoking that I will (as I did late last night for example) stop reading, grab a chair and walk out in front of my house, and just sit in the dark, a silent observer of all that is around me, listening to the crickets, looking into the sky. The Tao has that kind of effect on you; it makes you completely rethink everything that you do, say, and think. Never have I read anything that made me stop and think quite like the Tao Te Ching.

"Tao" means the way, "Te" means adding virtue to your life, and "Ching" means "book" in Chinese. It is based upon a book written over 2,500 years ago. According to tradition, it was written around 6th century BCE by the Taoist sage Laozi (or Lao Tzu, "Old Master"), a record-keeper at the Zhou Dynasty court, by whose name the text is known in China. They say that the Tao Te Ching is the manual for living. I share it here with you as merely an introduction and invite you to explore the 81 verses that comprise the Tao. You can read it in an afternoon, but you might end up studying for a lifetime. Books are available everywhere that will give you all 81 verses, and you can also go online and Google the Tao.

In my view, the Tao is not a religion, as some believe, but simply 81 verses of wisdom from a man who lived hundreds of years ago. To explore Taoism is to fully shift the way you live and think. When we get hungry for greater awareness of all things, a hunger for understanding ourselves, our actions and our behavior, it is then that we can have a massive shift in our thinking. I would submit to you that with this shift, we can begin to attract the events, people, and circumstances into our world that we desire.

So many people ignore their calling in life. Instead we listen to family or educational or religious institutions tell us how we should live. My own walk through life over the past several years has been about discovering my purpose, not about how much money I could make or how many things I could acquire. Obviously your purpose in life will be different from mine. Yours may be to magically strike a baseball thrown at you at over 98mph. Others may sense that their purpose is that of a teacher or a nurse, helping to educate and care for others. Some have talents in graphic design or computers, while others want to teach people to dance.

Whatever your purpose, it's critical that you explore what it is and not be afraid to pursue it, regardless of what you perceive as the risks. I would submit that when we do not walk with purpose in our lives, we cannot collide with our destiny.

The Tao contradicts almost everything that we have been taught in Western culture. If Western society tells us that we should strive to be rich, the Tao teaches that less is more; if modern Hollywood society, including bastions of "the look at me now" press, seems to paint a picture that you're really nobody unless you have been profiled in one of these celebrity rags, than the Tao reminds us that seeking acceptance and fame is not living a Tao existence.

The Tao reminds us that we came from nothing and will return to nothing; therefore why should we develop these oversized egos and feel that we are somehow so much more important than others who walk among us? Of course, our Western society mandates that we keep score against everyone. Thus you obsess about whether you drive a nicer car than your neighbor or your friend, whether your favorite college team or pro football team somehow let you down by not winning, whether you have a corner office with a window while everyone else is stuck working in a cubicle, feeling that these achievements somehow determine your self-worth. True enlightenment is being free of the opinions of others, thus completely directing the course of your life regardless of what others may think.

Answering your calling may, in other people's eyes, require that you take a risk. Reading each verse of the Tao Te Ching will make you question your calling. You will come to question, as I did, all the beliefs that you hold. Discovering the Tao has made me take a hard look at my ego, and at the destinations that I seek to arrive at. I submit to you that it will have you looking at and re-evaluating all that you hold dear.

During my darkest hours of life I could have used the wisdom of the Tao; unfortunately I would have to wait more than 19 years to find its healing words. It's been said that pain pushes us until vision guides us. With all that I have been through and all that I have lost, I have come to believe that losing ones sight would not be the worst thing to happen in life. It is our loss of vision of who we are, who we want to become and where we are going that is indeed a greater tragedy.

The Tao has brought me a sense of peace in a self-absorbed and highly competitive world; in fact it's made me rethink my own competitive nature. I want to share with you the verses that have struck a chord with me in the hopes that they will start you on your journey toward higher living and deeper thinking.

Verse 44 of the Tao states:

Which means more to you,
You or your renown?
Which brings more to you,
You or what you own?
I say what you gain
Is more trouble that what you lose.

Love is the fruit of sacrifice.
Wealth is the fruit of generosity.

A contented man is never disappointed.
He who knows when to stop is preserved from peril,
Only thus can you endure long.

This verse teaches us to understand the senselessness of being attached to material objects. We are trapped in a cycle of constantly striving and never arriving type mode. We try to find fulfillment in obtaining more things as opposed to looking within ourselves and finding contentment for who we are today. We must learn when enough is enough, when our cup is full, in everything from how much food we take in to how much money we accumulate.

Many of you know people who spend their entire life seeking more money, more friends, more places to go, more substances to abuse. This never ending cycle of more, more, more in essence becomes their jail. It's when we stop the vicious circle of chasing happiness through more stuff that we then become wealthy and feel more love, for the attainment of these false objects only serves to temporarily quench the ego's massive hunger for more attention and status. Living the Tao means coming to a place in your life in which you truly realize that less is more and all this stuff is not going to make your life perfect. Practice this 44th verse; practice stepping off the Hedonic Treadmill of more, more and more, and just practice being.

The 7th verse of the Tao states:

Heaven is eternal—the earth endures
Why do heaven and earth last forever?
They do not live for themselves only.
This is the secret of their durability.

For this reason the sage puts himself last
And so ends up ahead.
He stays a witness to life,
So he endures.

Serve the needs of others,
And all of your own needs will be fulfilled.
Through selfless action, fulfillment is attained.

This verse is great wisdom: give to others and in the process you indirectly give to yourself. When we encounter people in our daily walk through life who seek only to fend for themselves, to satiate their egos through drawing attention to their own activities, we see that in the long run, this behavior requires so much energy because what stands in its way is great opposition. The senior executive within the corporation who seeks only to protect his own turf will one day lose the very ground that he covets. He will do so because people don't respond to others that are selfish and egocentric. Recently a 58 year old senior executive with a large Fortune 500 company, someone I worked for in the early nineties, was fired. He was a senior vice president responsible for a large division in Southern California. After thirty years with this company he had the foundation pulled from underneath him in a very swift and decisive way. In one day his reality as he knew it was gone. He was never one to look out for others during his journey with this company, and like many who behave similarly, his journey came to a sudden stop. Why do some executives ascend to the top while others fade from view in the wake of a political struggle within the organization? I would submit that the reason for this kind of failure is self-centered behavior over a prolonged career. Much can be learned from the wisdom of this seventh verse.

The 33rd verse of the Tao states:

One who understands others has knowledge, one who understands himself has wisdom. Mastering others requires force; mastering the self needs strength.

If you realize that you have enough, you are truly rich.

One who gives himself to his position surely lives long.
One who gives himself to the Tao surely lives forever.

Most of us have encountered people who control our daily lives through force. Much has been written about management through intimidation and power. In my early and mid-twenties I was constantly haunted by overwhelming fear, always wondering if I was going to lose my job and face homelessness. Back then I had nowhere to turn, no family or significant savings. The funny thing was I was very capable and talented at my job, which back then was to be a successful sales and marketing person. I did those activities well and used my skill sets to the fullest, and yet I always lived with this fear.

There was a noticeable shift though in my thinking when I decided that I never wanted to master or control anyone. I made a conscious choice to not be controlling in relationships, and I certainly did not want to aspire to do this in business. People don't respond well to your attempts to control them; rather they end up building resentments towards you. If you are a CEO or you want to control and dominate your kids, keep in mind that over time you are building a cathedral of resentment in your subordinates or children. At some point, this cathedral will collapse and the wreckage will be the consequences. Better to interact with your kids and employees in a supportive way that helps them to build their character as opposed to trying to dominate them through force. Ultimately this will be futile.

The 17th verse of the Tao states:

With the greatest leader above them, people barely know one exists. Next comes one whom they love and praise. Next comes one whom they fear. Next comes one whom they despise and defy. When a leader trusts no one, no one trusts him.

The great leader speaks little. He never speaks carelessly. He works without self-interest and leaves no trace. When all is finished, the people say, "We did it ourselves."

Thousands of people have written thousands of books on management and leadership, and corporations have spent millions of dollars on training and seminars. I would submit that if people would simply take some time to raise their consciousness and follow the simple truths in the seventeenth verse of the Tao, life would be much simpler. Leaders of any group, organization or company can choose to lead with a loud, divisive voice of authority which ultimately leads employees to leave rather than be loyal. Enabling people within your company rather than controlling them will ultimately lead to greater results.

Verse 24 of the Tao states:

If you stand on tiptoe, you cannot stand firmly. If you take long steps, you cannot walk far. Showing off does not reveal enlightenment. Boasting will not produce accomplishment. He who is self-righteous is not respected. He who brags will not endure.
All these ways of acting are odious, distasteful. They are superfluous excesses. They are like a pain in the stomach, a tumor in the body.
When walking the path of the Tao, this is the very stuff that must be uprooted, thrown out, and left behind.

I learned this valuable lesson over many years. No one responds to those who have achieved much and then gone out of their way to make sure that you are aware of their prosperity. Instead, we must adopt a prosperity consciousness, which is to say that you can allow yourself to be successful. When we satiate our egos by throwing this success in the faces of others, we only build contempt along the way. It would be far better to use that energy to help those around you who are less fortunate than to show the world your preference for Louis Vuitton, Fendi, or Gucci which somehow separates you from the rest of society. If your dominant thoughts are for Mercedes and BMW instead of Africa and clean water, then you may want to reorganize your priorities. It is a natural desire to want to show the world that you have been successful, but the overwhelming need to do so will only keep you from higher living.

Verse 12 of the Tao states:

The five colors blind the eye.
The five tones deafen the ear.
The five flavors dull the taste.
The chase and the hunt craze people's minds.
Wasting energy to obtain rare objects only impedes
one's growth.
The master observes the world, but trusts his inner vision.
He allows things to come and go. He prefers what is
within to what is without.

Much of the Tao reflects on our modern society and its overwhelming need to chase objects. If it's not the paparazzi chasing celebrities in Hollywood, then it's us chasing that next fancy car or big house. It's the hunt for that promotion or prettier girlfriend. It is the desire for a slimmer body and enhanced chest that enables us to go under the knife and seek to augment what our creator has given to us. The energy that we use in satiating our need for bigger and better is at best ridiculous. At worst we become defined by what we drive, what we have or what we don't have, as if the man who drives an average car is not worthy of your attention and the man that drives the fancy Porsche somehow offers you a better life.

What is within us is always much more important than the things we enjoy or lack. Once we have come to understand this we will have achieved a level of enlightenment that will truly make our time on earth and our walk through life more peaceful and joyful.

THE TWENTY RULES FOR HIGHER LIVING

The Twenty Rules comprise my expanded version of *The Ten Rules for Being Human* by Cherie Carter-Scott.

- You will receive a body

- You will be presented with lessons

- There are no mistakes, only lessons

- Lessons are repeated until learned

- Learning does not end

- "There" is no better than "here"

- Others are only mirrors of you

- What you make of your life is up to you

- All the answers lie inside of you

- You will forget all of this at birth

- Failure is good; accept it, because it's how we learn

- Don't burn your bridges; the path in front of you may fall if you do

- Confront your fears; they will empower you

- Surround yourself with people who believe in you

- Choose to avoid negative people and drama in your life; you will live longer

- Don't be a victim of your past; if you do, it will keep you from your future

- Admit your mistakes and take responsibility for your behavior

- Don't waste days; you don't own tomorrow

- Search for something you love to do, or misery will find you

- Understand that you can achieve anything; it is all up to you.

WHAT IS THE PSYCHOLOGY OF HIGHER LIVING?

What Will Be Your Legacy?

The word "psychology" is the combination of two ideas: soul or mind (psyche) and study (-ology), meaning the study of the soul or mind. It can also be described as the science that deals with mental processes and behavior. There are numerous fields of psychology. Clinical psychology is concerned with diagnosing and treating disorders of the brain, emotional disturbances, and behavior problems. Child psychology is the study of the mental and emotional development of children and is part of developmental psychology, the study of changes in behavior that occur through the life span. Cognitive psychology deals with how the human mind receives and interprets impressions and ideas. Social psychology looks at how the actions of others influence the behavior of an individual.

The psychology of higher living as I have defined it is the most comprehensive study of how we go about the business of life. It encompasses what in our minds brings us to higher levels of awareness and enlightenment. As we have examined throughout this book, many people apply very little psychology to their lives. They move from day to day without much thought of what is required to live an extraordinary life. Many people have forgotten to apply self love to their life's equation. Adopting the psychology of higher living enables you to avoid accepting anything but the best in all facets of your life, from the food that you put into your temple and the relationships that you choose to engage in to the path that you walk as you explore your purpose for living. Once we have satiated our basic needs, we yearn to do something more with our life.

The thoughtless and never-ending cycle of personal consumption leaves us empty because it doesn't ask us how we can change the world, impact other lives and help many along the path. Transcending the lower forms of conscious-ness can allow us to become fully self-actualized, high per-forming and peaceful adults; this is a turning point in our lives. Hopefully in preceding chapters, we have brought a greater clarity to this process.

My message to people is simple: you only have one life. You can choose to remain a victim to the horrible things that may have happened to you in your life, or you can choose to gain strength from your setbacks and wisdom from the abuse you may have suffered. You can choose to stop feeling sorry for yourself and live the best life that you can. You can choose to bring peace, not chaos to yourself and others. Regardless of how bad your childhood was, or how many people may have hurt you, only you can choose to find good, healthy people to surround yourself with. These people will become the team that carries you through life. It is your choice to seek out the best that life has to offer. This is the path of enlightenment, of higher living.

It's amazing how much pain we bring upon our-selves. One of the most common ways we hurt ourselves is by driving while intoxicated. It's so easy to let this happen. You go out after work, have a couple of drinks with a friend and think nothing of it. Then you get in your car, and before you know it, you're being pulled over and arrested for driv-ing under the influence. Now you're stuck spending time in jail, losing your license, being handcuffed, spending thou-sands of dollars. Why? Because you needed to have a drink in front of your work mates, friends or clients. I am fortunate that this has never happened to me.

Many of us choose to be in dysfunctional and or abusive relationships. We have kids out of wedlock, or we choose to not eat healthy or be physically active. We choose to smoke, then wonder why we're dying from lung cancer in our fifties. All of these things are choices, every day. What most people forget in life is that we really can live the life that we want to live. It's our choice. The other option is to live in the past, blaming our parents or past accidents and unexpected deaths for the way our life is today. We choose to throw one big pity party for ourselves. Many people are so caught up in the drama of their lives, drama that they have created, that they miss out on some of life's simple daily pleasures.

My daily pleasure is getting my morning mocha and taking Bosco for his walk. The primary things that bring pleasure and fulfillment to my life are playing in weekly tennis matches, helping others go from renting an apartment to owning their dream home, having nice dinners, renting a bike for a long ride along the beach, sleeping in on Sundays, connecting with people who are less fortunate or need intervention, and speaking to people, corporations and groups, sharing stories that will help them. I believe it is the setbacks of my life and the many people who have tragically left me that help me to recognize life's routine and simple pleasures.

As a corporate executive, it is imperative that you think about what kind of environment that you foster for your employees. Sometimes the politics of the corporate world are just as crazy and ridiculous as the politics of high school. We all remember high school don't we? Were we one of the cool kids, part of the "in-crowd?" Or did we feel like outsiders, lost and lonely away from others? In the 1960s, you would typically have one career for twenty years. Now, you're more likely to switch jobs and even careers five to seven times in a lifetime. Is all of that necessary? If more companies enabled their employees to prosper at higher levels, we might not see the incredible amounts of turnover that we see today. If you're a CEO, ask yourself this question: what is it that people want from their jobs or careers? I think I have the answer. Mostly, people want autonomy, freedom and unlimited opportunity, both financially and otherwise. Sadly, very few companies provide that today. It's your choice; it's your company. You can decide to create a family-like environment that gives people a chance to be their absolute best, or you can be like most companies, trudging along, rehiring, and retraining new people year in and year out.

My message would not be complete without a special word to parents. If you think that providing a roof over your kid's head and some basic food and clothing is going to result in a productive member of society, you're probably wrong. Strong words to be sure. It might be enough. The bare minimum was enough in my case, but not without a lot of pain and hard work. In most cases it falls woefully short. A moment of passion is no excuse to sentence a child to a life without love, guidance, protection, and education. And, if you think that sending your kid to public schools is the only education that little Johnny needs, you're dead wrong. Education is much more than just school. According to America's Promise Alliance, 1.2 million kids drop out of high school annually in the United States, never receiving their diploma. In Detroit Michigan, the graduation rate for high school kids is a mere 24.9%.

Let me give you an idea of what a better education might look like. It would start with a trip to the morgue. No, that's not a misprint. How do you expect a sixteen year old to get behind the wheel of a four thousand pound missile and expect him or her to guide it safely on a daily basis? Teenage kids have no real knowledge of how lethal that weapon really is, or how deadly the consequences of their mistakes can be. After the morgue, I also suggest attending an AA meeting or two with your child, and taking a trip to the ER. It's imperative that we take teenagers out of their music, their skin problems, dating woes, and clothes and move them into reality, even if only for a few hours. Who knows, it may just save your kid's life.

As I turn the final pages on this book, I am haunted on this night, as I am on many by the question that one must ask if we are to indeed live our greatest life. What will be my legacy, what will be your legacy? The intrinsic value of our lives cannot be measured by the totality of just our actions, nor can they be measured by what we have accumulated. Looking back over the landscape of my own life, and as a witness to many others who have lived extraordinary lives, I often reflect on people such as my friend Mathew. As a child growing up, my mother and his mother were best friends. Many days of my youth were spent at Joan's house. Sadly, Joan passed away at the age of only 53, two short years after my mother. She had been in a car accident. Mathew went on and lived quite a spectacular life. He was an elementary school teacher by day, but with summers off he traveled the world.

I knew he enjoyed mountain climbing and hiking, and had a thirst for the outdoors, another place at some far off corner of the world. My last visit to see Mathew in 1999 was so joyous, and yet so very brief. His infectious smile greeted me this one last time, and he invited me in. We sat and talked about the wonderful memories of our mom's. He was packing his bags and getting ready for another trip to Europe.

Mathew traveled widely for several years, particularly in Europe and Asia. He worked for a number of those years as a teacher at a summer camp in Rolle, Switzerland, on Lake Geneva. He was an assistant English teacher in Paris, harvested grapes in Bordeaux and was an interpreter during the Reagan-Gorbachev summit talks in Geneva. He spoke both French and Spanish.

During his trips to Europe, he spent much of his free time mountain climbing in Chamonix-Mt. Blanc in France. He had climbed mountains in Mexico, Argentina, Ecuador, Peru, Tanzania, France and Wales, among other locations. His major climbs included Mt. Blanc, in Chamonix, France; Aconcaqua, in Argentina; Mt. McKinley, in Alaska, and Mt. Kilimanjaro, in Tanzania. Mathew met his wife through mutual climbing friends. He proposed on Valentine's Day of 2000 during a hike up Mt. Baldy in the snow. They were married in October of that year, and traveled to Africa during their honeymoon to climb Mt. Kilimanjaro.

Suddenly, as I have done on so many late nights, as the night turned into early morning, I staggered to my computer as Mathew entered my consciousness. It had been a while since we last spoke and I wondered why he had not responded to a note that I had left for him. I entered his name into a yahoo search and was devastated to see that his obituary popped into my screen.

Matthew James Richardson, 40, died June 24, 2002 along with two climbing partners when a formation of glacial ice, created an avalanche near the summit on Mt. Huascar, the tallest mountain peak in Peru.

What an extraordinary life this man led. As I slumped in the chair I was numb with grief and sadness. For he had done what so many of us fail to do, he had found his passion, was living on purpose and exploring the world at a feverish pace. He lived more in 40 years than many of us live over a lifetime.

At the other end of the spectrum, of the many people that have come in and out of my life, only one has lived what

I deem to be the most fullest of lives, my dear friend Steven Peck. From his youth as a Hollywood actor and dancer starring alongside Frank Sinatra and Dean Martin, to teaching the wife of Elvis, Priscilla Presley, to dance, to owning one of the most successful restaurants I ever seen, Steve lived every one of his 76 years to the fullest. My last time with him was joyous. I had taken him and his wife to the Hollywood Bowl. Even as cancer had set in, he was triumphant and vigorous to the end. A few weeks passed, and I received a call that the end was near. Steve was taken home for his final visit and was now in his living room, unconscious, but resting peacefully. With his family gathered by his bedside, I knelt down to clutch his hand. He was in his final hour of life and the pain for me was overwhelming. I felt so honored to be with a man in his final moments. He had spent many months of each year, traveling the countryside of Europe, being free to explore the world and his love of wine. His appetite for people was infectious. This was evidenced several days later as more than 300 people gathered to say goodbye. But for now, I could only think how wonderful it was that he was surrounded by a family that loved and treasured him as did I. After I left, his wife said that at the moment his heart gave out and he took his last breath, a glorious rainbow had appeared through the living room window, as if his soul had been lifted.

To that end, I wish you the very best on your journey. My hope is that you will leave your dark valleys behind and reach the glory that is the mountaintop; in doing so you will achieve the ultimate in higher living.

We learn some things from prosperity, but we learn many more from adversity.

Dedicated to the Loving Memory of Nancy Lee

Though I walked into your room one last time and saw an ugly, senseless death, I will choose to remember you not as how I found you that dreadful day, but as the beautiful woman and mother that you are. Your death only serves to give me strength. Your memory only serves to give me wisdom and hope. May God bless you and keep you until such time that I am lucky enough to see you again. Until that day I will promise to touch as many people as I can so that they may learn from your tragic death.

In Loving Memory Of
Craig Andrew

Craig,

May God have mercy on my soul, for your memory burns inside mine every day. Though I may walk in the shadow of your death, I will carry your memory for all the days of my life. My promise to you is that people will learn from my mistake, and your life will not have been in vain. In an instant my careless mistake sent you away, but I will honor your memory by helping to save others. I would give anything to bring you back and reunite you with your family.

You were my best friend and I truly loved you as my brother. I will never forget the time that I first met you, picked you up and drove you home in the rain. From that day forward we were friends. But our days were too few. We were just kids then, so full of life, our futures in front of us. I know your mother, brother, sister, girlfriend and father loved you. Everyone who met you did— you were so full of life, and you had such a big smile. May you dwell in the house of the Lord, where pain and sorrow are no more, but life is everlasting.

ABOUT THE AUTHOR:

THE INSTITUTE FOR HUMAN DEVELOPMENT

Glenn Gary is the founder and president of The Institute for Human Development, a non-profit organization created to affect change and save lives in Africa. In an effort to bring clean drinking water and address the scourge of malnutrition that is killing thousands of children daily, he created Project Africa.

As a voice of reason in a society of increasingly confused values, The Institute for Human Development serves as a springboard for people that desire greater awareness and the ability to make a contribution to a cause greater than their own. To that end, the primary mission of the institute is two fold.

1) Be a gathering place for people to hear a positive message, engage in a deeper conversation of the life issues that all of us face. Learn to adopt healthier choices that result in helping people overcome addictions, fight obesity, unlock from toxic relationships and develop a greater purpose for their lives.

2) Raise money for the development of Project Africa. According to the U.S. Department of State, more than 1.1 billion people lack access to safe drinking water; 2.6 billion people – almost half the total population in developing countries - lack access to proper sanitation. On any given day, approximately 50% of the world's hospital beds are filled with patients suffering from water and sanitation related diseases. Each year 1.8 million children in developing countries die from diarrhea disease - the second leading cause of death after pneumonia. Globally, diarrhea kills at least as many people as tuberculosis or malaria, and five times more children than HIV/AIDS. The situation in Africa is particularly bleak. In 27 African countries, greater than 30% of the population does not have access to safe water. In nine of those countries, more than 50% of the people lack access to safe water.

Beyond their direct public health consequences, inadequate water supply and sanitation are especially important issues for women and girls. In Mozambique, rural Senegal, and eastern Uganda, the UN reports that women spend on average 15-17 hours per week collecting water – often walking 6 miles or more in the dry season. Each dollar spent on water and sanitation yields $8 dollars of benefits in saved time, increased productivity, and reduced health costs. Beyond the numbers, increased access to water and sanitation would improve education, empower women, promote human dignity and reduce the pain and suffering associated with high child mortality rates.

If you desire to make a mark on the world, we ask you to gather with us each week and unite on a mission of change. Our initial goal is to raise $1 million dollars in an effort to save lives and bring clean drinking water to people in Africa. In addition, our mission is to provide a place where people can gather to hear a powerful, uplifting and positive message.

Glenn is also the founder of Glenn Gary International, Inc., a multinational speaking, consulting and training firm that works with corporations and individuals to help them reach their peak performance. He has been speaking to professional and trade groups, corporations and associations for over twenty-one years.

Prior to forming the Institute for Human Development, Glenn Gary started his first successful cleaning business at the age of just eighteen. Since then, he has successfully launched two companies and pursued successful careers in sales and marketing, real estate investing, consulting, and mortgage banking. In addition, for ten years, he ran his own investment banking and mergers & acquisitions firm. Throughout his diverse career Glenn has spoken to thousands of people from various groups and coached many individuals for peak performance. His speaking programs are as diverse as his twenty-one year business career and include:

The Psychology of Higher Living
Women's Health Alert
Turning Setbacks into Success
Mastering Your Future
A Winning Attitude is Everything
Becoming A Million Dollar Manager
The 20 Rules for Living
Sell or Die: a World Class Selling and Training Program
The War Plan for High Achievement Selling
Wall Street Riches

Glenn is the accomplished author of two other books, *Wall Street Riches* and *To Sell or Die*, all published by OakStreet Press www.oakstreetpress.com.

In his latest book, *To Sell or Die, The Dualistic Nature of Your Company & Why Its Costing You Millions*, Glenn takes a critical look at how Fortune 500 and small companies alike are losing millions by not enabling their people to have unmitigated income opportunities. The book examines what company leaders, management and CEO's can do to change their corporate culture and increase their profits dramatically.

Glenn Gary has also created a 15 title cd audio library, some of which are available on Itunes. Titles of Glenn's audio cd's include:

Creating Wealth
Finding Your Purpose in Life
Identity Theft
Are You The Woman You Want To Be
Creating Powerful Relationships
Are Addictions Killing You
Healthy Body/Healthy Life
Teen Drinking, Killer on The Road
Starting A Business
Life After Divorce
Life Goals & Time Management
Living The Tao
Mortgage Secrets Revealed
How Credit Works & How To Fix It
Nine Principles of Success

If you find yourself, your company or organization "deep in a valley" and struggling to reach the mountaintop, contact Glenn to book a speaking engagement, keynote, coaching session or training program. If you are a meeting planner or would like more information on Glenn and how his speaking programs can be custom tailored to fit your audience, please visit Glenn Gary International at www.glenspeaking.com

The Institute for Human Development
Glenn Gary International, Inc.
888-242-5852
Email: glenn@glenspeaking.com

endfatigne.com
"Remember" (dementia)
methyline blue